THE WATERS OF MORMON

A NOVEL OF ALMA THE ELDER

ROBERT H. MOSS

Library of Congress No.: 86-081775
ISBN: 0-88290-285-7
Horizon Publishers Catalog & Order No.: 1969
First Printing, 1986

Printed and distributed
in the United States of America by

Horizon
Publishers
& Distributors, Incorporated
50 South 500 West P.O. Box 490
Bountiful, Utah 84010-0490

Preface

Alma's story, more than anything else, is a story of repentance. Great men throughout ages were called upon to repent before receiving rights of leadership. In Alma's case, we can only guess the extent of his sins, but we know the depth of his repentance. He became one of the greatest spiritual leaders of the entire Book of Mormon.

An interesting character in Alma's story is Abinadi, the prophet. Who was he? Where did he come from? Where did he receive his great scriptural understanding? Abinadi was Alma's forerunner as John the Baptist was the Savior's. Without him, or someone like him, there probably would have been no Alma story. For forerunners like Abinadi many generations are thankful.

An important element in each book in the Nephite Chronicles series has been the father—son relationship: Jacob and Joseph, Lehi and Nephi, now Alma and his sons. This book is dedicated to fathers everywhere. May it influence your choices as you help your sons grow to manhood.

One man said that great men are only ordinary men who commit themselves and accomplish extraordinary things. The chroniclers of the Book of Mormon were great men who accomplished extraordinary things. Each carried forth traditions begun by his ancestor, Joseph; learned to write complicated Egyptian hieroglyphics and Hebrew script. These books depict the characteristics of which heroes are made.

Contents

Prologue

Nephi's descendants delighted in the Land of Lehi-Nephi. The soil was rich, climate ideal, and all natural resources were available for happy prosperous living. Stone and stucco homes and temples abounded in the land, replacing the log buildings of Nephi's time. Temple and palace facades displayed beautiful, intricate carvings.

With few exceptions peace reigned in the Land of Nephi until after Jacob's death. Then for two-hundred-fifty years the Nephites came under increasingly violent Lamanite attacks. Valiant kings led Nephites in battle defending their lands from Lamanite hordes who "loved murder and would drink the blood of beasts." Thousands of Nephites and Lamanites were slain. Throughout this period the prophets continued to warn the people that unless they lived according to the commandments they would be destroyed.

A dynasty of scribes, schooled in Hebrew and Egyptian languages, preserved records and passed responsibility from father to son. The small plates of Nephi were passed through eight generations of scribes: Nephi to Jacob, to Enos, Jarom, Omni, Amaron, Chemish, Abinadom, and Amaleki. After Amaleki the small plates were combined with the large plates kept by King Mosiah's scribes.

Lamanite aggressiveness increased. The Lord commanded King Mosiah to take his people and move from the Land of Nephi to another land which would be shown him. Mosiah—reminiscent of Abraham, Moses, Lehi and Nephi—hearkened to the Lord's voice. His people packed their belongings and left beautiful homes and cities to go to another "promised land." For them the move was one of great sadness. For generations their forefathers had dwelled in the Land of Nephi. Tears flowed freely as Mosiah's people trudged away from the land of their inheritance.

Descending from the beauty of the mountain valleys of the Land of Nephi to the jungle hotlands in the north, they cut their way through forests and almost inpenetrable jungles. King Mosiah, guided by the Lord, led them onward.

After a month's wandering, the Nephites were led to the Land of Zarahemla which was inhabited by a people who left Jerusalem a few years after the departure of Lehi and his family. With this people came Mulek, young son of King Zedekiah. From him they took their name. The

Mulekites were a numerous people, but with no written records their language had deteriorated so much that Mosiah's people could not understand them.

Mosiah instructed his scribes to teach the Mulekites the Nephite language. Soon the two peoples united and chose Mosiah as king. The combined peoples dwelt in peace until the end of his righteous reign.

Upon King Mosiah's death, Benjamin, Mosiah's son, was appointed king. Benjamin lived close to the Lord. During his kingship the Lamanites, bitter enemies of the Nephites, discovered the Land of Zarahemla and again wars raged.

Many people, intrigued by stories told by ancestors concerning the land of their first inheritance, longed to return to that land. A large Nephite group departed Zarahemla to return to the Land of Nephi. Torn by contention, this first expedition failed. Fifty of the original group survived and made their way back to Zarahemla.

A second group, led by righteous Zeniff, tried again. Lehi, with his wife, Karla, and small son, Abimolam, joined the expedition. Lehi, descendant of Nephi, was brother of Amaleki, the last scribe of the small plates of Nephi. Like Amaleki, Lehi had been schooled as a scribe. Zeniff asked him to be scribe of their expedition.

Arriving in the Land of Nephi, Zeniff entered into an agreement with Laman, the Lamanite king: Nephites might possess the city of Lehi-Nephi and Land of Shilom. Zeniff and the Nephites thrilled to be where ancestors had lived. The land was as beautiful as they had been told. They loved the peacefulness of mountains, clear mountain lakes, and delightful climate. They were a happy people.

For more than a decade, Zeniff's people peacefully planted and harvested crops and built up the city. Lehi, the record-keeper, faithfully kept chronicles of the people.

The Lamanites, threatened by the industriousness and growth of Zeniff's people, came against them in battle. Righteous Nephites, with the Lord's help, overcame the Lamanites and dwelt in uneasy peace for a few more years.

Abimolam, Lehi's son, learned to be a scribe. He was righteous and enjoyed a close relationship with the Lord. When Abimolam was twenty, King Zeniff appointed him as a priest. In that capacity, he was often in the palace. He fell in love with Marji, King Zeniff's daughter. They were married and in the four hundred and twenty-sixth year after Lehi and his family left Jerusalem, a son was born to them. They named him Alma. Three years later, his mother gave birth to a little girl. Alma's mother developed complications and both mother and daughter died.

As a priest's son, Alma had many privileges. Following traditions of his fathers he trained as a scribe, learning to write both Hebrew and Egyptian. He was baptized by his father, and, at the age of thirteen, was ordained to the priesthood.

When Alma was fourteen his grandfather, King Zeniff, died. His uncle Noah became king. Noah, a big, swarthy man with heavy eyebrows and deep-set eyes, was not like his father, Zeniff. His youth had been spent in riotous living and now he was king. One of Noah's first official acts was to rid himself of all the faithful priests his father had appointed. In their places he appointed men as priests whom he could control.

Abimolam, heartsick over his removal from the priesthood, aged quickly. He and Alma lived alone in poverty. Their only income came from the few jobs he was able to find as a scribe. They raised a garden and lived off produce. Times were difficult and Abimolam's bitterness infected Alma, who vowed he would never live in poverty and privation again.

King Noah had his eye on his youthful nephew. He called him to the palace. Apparently pleased with the twenty-year-old Alma, Noah appointed him as one of his priests.

Abimolam attempted to convince Alma to decline the appointment, but Alma would not listen. Being part of Noah's court was what he had schemed for. He knew how the priests lived. He had seen their fine houses and embroidered clothing. Now *he* could live the life of luxury. His father, Abimolam, had complained of how Noah taxed people heavily to pay for elegant buildings, wine vineyards and concubines, but Alma didn't care. He just wanted to get his share of wealth. Now he had fulfilled his desire.

When twenty-two, Alma married Esther, a maid in the king's court. This is their story.

Chapter 1

Abinadi

Shouting, angry voices—voices of scorn raised above the market place babble—drew Esther's attention. The familiar smells—spices, hot bread, and frying meat—were there, but never had the market place seemed so crowded or so noisy. Raucous laughter and derisive shouts echoed back and forth along plastered walls. Esther passed booths of cured skins and meat—booths where carcasses of rabbits, turkey, deer, armadillo, peccary and iguana hung in various stalls. She kept looking curiously towards the crowd formed on one end of the square. What was the commotion? She shivered in the cool air and pulled her shawl tightly around her.

Curiosity won. Squeezing into the crowd she caught a glimpse of what had attracted the throng. She was disappointed. Standing before them, his back to the wall, surrounded by market-goers, was a skinny, older man in ragged clothes. His hair, white and thinning, was in tangled disarray. Esther moved closer, her attention attracted to the man's thin face. The eyes! That was it. Above his hawk nose, his eyes were bright and alive, almost searing with their intensity. They bored into the faces of his tormentors, moving slowly from one to another. When those eyes met hers she felt a burning within her. She didn't understand this feeling and moved even closer.

The hecklers' voices died, allowing her to hear the man speak. His voice was high-pitched, yet with a strong timbre like her husband's. There was a compelling quality to it. Esther listened intently.

Hands raised towards the heavens, he shouted, "The Lord has told me to tell you, 'Wo be unto you, for I have seen your abominations, and your wickedness, and your whoredoms, and except you repent I will visit you in mine anger.' "

His voice was lost in the hostile crowd's angry response. Esther strained to hear. Turning to a woman beside her, she asked,

"Who is this man?"

"He gave his name as Abinadi."

Abinadi's words continued. "Except this people repent and turn unto God they shall be brought into bondage and none shall deliver them."

14

A tingling ran up Esther's spine. For some reason she believed this man. She listened carefully to every word, and when he was through speaking and had slipped off through the crowd, she tried to recall his phrases. Words repeated themselves in her mind as she shopped from booth to booth. "The Lord will not hear their prayers." "He will be slow to hear their cries." "I will let them be smitten by their enemies."

Esther purchased dried fish and acorn squash for supper. Finishing her marketing as quickly as possible she made her way home through busy streets. She pondered Abinadi's words while she cooked dinner.

Alma arrived home from the palace as she sliced mangoes for dessert. He looked preoccupied, gave her a quick kiss on the cheek, and went back outside. The scent of palm wine lingered in the air behind him.

Esther sighed. Alma has surely not been paying much attention to me lately, she thought. She hoped rumors she had heard about King Noah giving each of his priests several concubines were untrue. She gritted her teeth and stifled tears which threatened to flow.

"Oh, Alma," she whispered, "please don't let it be true."

She called her family for dinner. Zoram, their son, ran excitedly into the room. She smiled tenderly at him. At two years he seemed to be into everything. He chased butterflies, collected pretty rocks, climbed trees, and did many things to cause her to worry. Now he reached out and put his arms around her knees.

Esther smiled and patted him on the head, then knelt down and drew him to her. Held-back tears escaped, and Zoram pulled back.

"Mamma, why you cry?"

"It's just that I love you very much," she replied huskily.

The answer seemed to satisfy him, and he again ran from her. In a few minutes he returned, his hand in his father's. Alma had a tender smile. Esther knew of his feelings for their first-born son.

She served their food, then sat back and watched them eat. As they ate, she indulged in a favorite pastime, studying Alma. The man she had married was tall. His thick black hair and beard were well-trimmed. Heavy black eyebrows made him look as if he were frowning until one saw the twinkle in his deep-set dark eyes. Esther had to admit that those eyes could be hard one moment and laughing the next. His nose was large and aquiline. Above his firm chin his lips were full and warm. She smiled as she looked at him. Very warm, she thought.

Alma sat back with a sigh. "Thank you. That was delightful."

Esther cleaned up from the meal, then she timidly approached her husband in his study. "Alma?" He looked at her, a slight frown on his face.

Esther took his hands. "Alma, there was the strangest man in the market today."

"Oh. What of him?"

Her words tumbled out unrestrained. "He spoke about our people's wickedness and the anger of God and called people to repentance."

Alma laughed. "And who is this beggar, that we should listen to him?"

Esther whispered, a faraway look in her eye. "His name is Abinadi. I believe he speaks truth. I believe he is really a prophet."

Angrily, Alma rose, his eyes hard and flinty. "So he has filled you with his lies. I say away with him. Tomorrow I will personally tell King Noah of this man and his insurrection."

Next morning Alma had his audience with the king. Noah sat on a raised dais at the end of a huge throne room. Walls were decorated with ziff: cedar-wood designs, overlaid with gold, brass and silver. The patterned cedar was exquisite, and by highlighting carvings with shining metal, it was even more striking.

The sybaritic king sat spraddle-legged, with his enormous stomach protruding onto his legs. A scantily-clad girl knelt before him polishing the nails on his left hand. His right hand held a goblet of wine. Another girl sat beside him feeding him tiny boiled shrimp with her fingers. The king, with a casual wave of his goblet, motioned Alma to speak.

Alma rehearsed to him what Esther had seen and heard at the market. "Abinadi is accusing us of all kinds of wickedness."

"Who is this Abinadi that he should judge us?" the king sneered. Then in a mocking voice, "And who is this God that shall bring such great affliction upon my people?"

Lids half covering his weak and crafty eyes, he leaned forward and grasped the arms of his gilded throne. "And why do you bring this news?"

Alma bowed again before Noah. "This man is no ordinary rabble-rouser, my king. He also talked about you. He said your life would not be worth more than a cloak thrown into a hot furnace."

Noah's temper flared. He pushed away the girls, gave his goblet to a servant, and half rose to his feet. His hands gripped the chair's arms so tightly his knuckles were white from the strain. He called his guards and instructed them to find Abinadi.

"Bring this Abinadi here," he hissed. "For stirring our people to rebellion this man deserves to die."

* * *

Abinadi had disappeared. Noah's guards searched the entire city. The white-haired prophet was not to be found. Rainy season followed dry season, and Abinadi was mostly forgotten. Some, like Esther, secretly attempted to remember his words.

Alma, walking through the city, reflected on his assignment. As King Noah's priest he was always busy. There was so much form and pageantry, so many social events that required his presence. Then there were his concubines. He sighed audibly. I have not desired concubines, he thought, but what was I to do when Noah gave them to me?

He was on his way to visit Rebecca, his favorite concubine. A twinge of guilt made him duck his head. His life with Esther was good. She made him happy and had presented him with a son. He smiled as he thought of her. Esther's long shiny brown hair was usually tied back in a bun or wrapped in a colorful scarf. He loved the way her blue-gray eyes crinkled as she laughed. He sighed as he thought of her small pert nose and soft warm lips.

Her skin was so soft. He had teased her about the milky cactus juice she rubbed into her skin each night. He shrugged. It must work.

He tore his thoughts back to his present mission. Having several concubines held no excitement, but was something Noah wanted his priests to do. And, he thought somewhat smugly, as Noah's youngest priest I don't want anything to jeopardize my position.

His thoughts were interrupted by a commotion ahead. Sandals slapped on the hardened dirt street as he ran into the square. He pushed his way into the crowd.

"What is it? What has happened?"

"Some old man preaching," was the laconic reply.

Alma stopped and listened.

"I will cause that they shall have burdens lashed upon their backs; and they shall be driven before like a dumb ass."

"Who's he talking about?" Alma whispered.

"Us."

" . . . and it shall come to pass that except they repent I will utterly destroy them from off the face of the earth."

Alma had heard all he wanted to hear. He was indignant. How dare this man preach against the people? He pushed his way forward.

"Move aside, I am a priest of King Noah." He roughly elbowed his way until he stood facing the man who had been speaking.

The speaker, tall and gaunt, stood before him. The man was probably about fifty years of age, but looked older. Alma could see the deeply-etched lines written in the man's sun-darkened face. They told of exhaustion and endless privations. His once black hair was thin and heavily silvered. The eyes which burned out of that thin face were dark and glowing and intense. Alma shuddered. They seemed hypnotic: the eyes of a madman inspired by fanatical dedication.

Alma started forward but stopped transfixed, listening.

The old man looked deeply into Alma's eyes and continued sadly, "The Lord commanded me, saying, *Abinadi, go and prophesy unto this, my people, for they have hardened their hearts against my words. They have not repented of their evil doings, therefore, I will visit them in my anger. Yea, in my fierce anger will I visit them in their iniquities and abominations."*

The words engraved themselves into Alma's memory. His spirit burned within him. Was it possible that this man could actually be a prophet? The words rang of sincerity and truth. Perhaps Noah's priests were wrong. What would that mean?

He had to do something. The crowd knew he was a priest. His duty was to arrest this man and bring him before the council. He steeled himself to do that when a disturbance at the crowd's rear turned all heads.

Oh no! Alma wished he could hide. Coming toward him were Nakka and Tay, two fellow priests, and they had several guards with them.

Now he had no choice. He stepped forward and grabbed Abinadi's arm. "The king has given instructions that you be brought before him on charges of inciting the people to riot." Alma was surprised at the hardness of the arm he held. "Who are you who dares speak against our king?"

"My name is Abinadi," the prophet responded calmly. "What I have said about the king will come true. Noah's life will be of no more value than a silken garment in a hot furnace. Thus saith the Lord."

Obviously, Nakka and Tay heard the last statement. Nakka struck the back of his hand across Abinadi's face. Blood spurted from his nose, but eyes looked calmly at his attackers. Sadly, Abinadi's head moved almost imperceptibly from side to side. Alma flinched inside.

The crowd cheered as guards tied the hands of unprotesting Abinadi behind his back. Then, with a rope around his neck, they dragged him down the street. Alma walked with the priests for several blocks, then watched as the figures moved towards the king's palace. His feelings were very confused.

The concubine, Rebecca, was forgotten. Alma made his solitary way home. Thoughts raced through his mind. If Abinadi's words were true, and he almost believed they were, then the beliefs Noah's priests had taught him were false. All were justifications for excesses they had been living. Was his father right after all? His face burned with shame as he thought of things he had done. Can I repent? How? I must talk to Abinadi.

Esther met him at the door. He kissed her but his mind was elsewhere. He walked into his study and pulled a dusty parchment from a bin. The parchment was a copy of the scriptures his father had given him. He had not read any of them for years.

He sat by the window, open scroll before him. His eyes skimmed through the writings until his attention was attracted to the words of Isaiah.

"How beautiful upon the mountains are the feet of him that bringeth good tidings; that publisheth peace; that bringeth good tidings of good; that publisheth salvation; that saith unto Zion, Thy God Reigneth."

There was more. He read the scripture carefully. He was reading the chapter for the third time when Esther came into the room.

"There's a messenger at the door."

Alma said, "Have him come in."

He recognized the boy, a court page.

"What is it?"

The page bowed. "The king has commanded all priests to gather for a council to determine the fate of Abinadi, the so-called prophet."

Alma nodded. With a wave he dismissed the boy.

He rolled up the parchment, stuck it under his arm, then bid goodbye to Esther. By the time he arrived at the palace, the other priests were already in place. He slipped into his seat in the back row while King Noah was still instructing them.

"This man is a trouble-maker. He has attempted to stir up our people to rebellion. Question him, then pass sentence."

Alma knew what sentence the king would demand.

Abinadi, hands and ankles fettered with chain, stood before the priests. Alma recoiled as he saw bruises where the old man had been beaten. Abinadi stood, unbowed, dignified even in chains. Alma looked around, noting glances of hatred on faces of his fellow priests. Helam, Alma's friend, had a look of rapt interest.

Noah's priests threw questions at Abinadi with intent to cross him, but he answered boldly. Alma smiled inwardly. Abinadi was keen-witted. He turned questions intended as snares back to the questioners, obviously confusing and embarrassing the priests.

Alma's turn finally came. He unrolled his parchment and asked, "What do these words mean which have been written by our fathers: 'How beautiful upon the mountains are the feet of him that bringeth good tidings . . . ?' " Alma read the entire passage, then looked at Abinadi. He asked again, "What does it mean?"

Abinadi spread his arms as wide as the chain allowed. He looked with disdain at the priests.

"Are you priests and pretend to teach this people, and don't even know what the words of the prophets mean? Wo unto you for perverting the word of the Lord."

Malik, one of the younger priests, responded, "We cannot teach what we don't understand."

"Even if you understood these things, you have not taught them. You have not applied your hearts to understanding. You have not been wise. If you don't understand the scriptures, what have you taught this people?"

Amulon, the chief priest, said tartly, "We have taught the Law of Moses."

"If you teach the Law of Moses why do you not live it yourselves? Why do you commit whoredoms and spend your strength with harlots?"

He looked up at the priests, many of whom averted their eyes.

He nodded sadly. "Yes, you know that I speak the truth." He looked directly at Amulon, the chief priest. "You have said you teach the Law of Moses. What do you know about the Law of Moses? Does salvation come by the Law of Moses?"

Raising himself out of his seat, Amulon, his eyes squinted in anger, replied. "Yes!" he almost shouted. "Salvation does come by the Law of Moses!"

Abinadi continued quietly. "If you keep the commandments of God you shall be saved."

Amulon hissed, "And what commandments do you speak of, old man?"

"The commandments which the Lord delivered unto Moses in the Mount of Sinai: *I am the Lord thy God who hath brought thee out of the land of Egypt, out of the house of bondage. Thou shalt have no other God before me. Thou shalt not make unto thee any graven image, or any likeness of any thing in heaven above, or things which are in the earth below.*"

Again he eyed the priests. "Have you done this? No, you have not. Have you taught the people these commandments? No, you have not."

The king had seemed to be listening intently, anger showing on his face. Now his patience apparently ended. He pointed a pudgy finger at Abinadi.

"Away with this fellow! We have heard enough! He is a madman." He clapped his hands. "Guards. Take this man and execute him."

The guards stepped towards the condemned man.

Abinadi turned, his eyes blazing. Stretching forth his arms, he cried, "Do not touch me or you will die! I have not yet delivered the message which God sent me to deliver."

He looked directly at King Noah. "You say I am mad because I tell you the truth about yourselves."

As Alma looked, Abinadi's countenance seemed to shine. Alma was further convinced that Abinadi was a prophet.

With power which held the guards immobilized, Abinadi continued. "King Noah, you have no power to slay me until I have finished my message." His eyes narrowed. "After I have given you this message, it won't matter what you do to me. But listen carefully. Whatever you do to me will be a pattern of what will befall you."

The priests fidgeted nervously as he looked at them. "I see that what I have said angers you," he said. "So be it. Your guilt condemns you before God."

On the back row, Alma listened with rapt attention. As Abinadi continued, he dipped his brush and began taking careful notes. "I told you that the Lord commanded that *Thou shalt not make any graven image.* Now I will give the rest of the commandments of God. *Thou shalt not bow down thyself unto them, nor serve them; for I thy Lord am a jealous God.*

Thou shalt not take the name of the Lord thy God in vain, for the Lord will not hold him guiltless that taketh his name in vain. Remember the Sabbath day to keep it holy. Six days shalt thou labor and do all thy work. Honor thy father and thy mother, that thy days may be long upon the land which the Lord thy God giveth thee.

Thou shalt not kill.

Thou shalt not commit adultery.

Thou shalt not steal.

Thou shalt not bear false witness against thy neighbor.

Thou shalt not covet."

Alma wrote Abinadi's words, his guilt intensified. Each commandment Abinadi pointed out applied to his life. He listened attentively as Abinadi talked of the law and its application to this people. Then Abinadi quoted words of Isaiah, words Alma had just read in his scrolls.

Abinadi read of a "man of sorrows, and acquainted with grief." After quoting the whole passage, and apparently noting the vacant look upon the faces of the uncomprehending priests, he clarified what he had quoted.

"The words I have given you tell us that God himself shall come to the earth and will dwell among men. He will be called the Son of God and will subject His flesh to the will of the Father."

Alma wrote quickly, ignoring the side glances of fellow priests. Abinadi talked about this God who would come to earth; who would suffer temptation without yielding; would work many miracles; would be slain by his own people; and then would break the bonds of death and ascend again into heaven. The words were beautiful and Alma's bosom seemed on fire. He knew Abinadi spoke the truth.

Then Abinadi talked of redemption of the Son of God. He spoke of resurrection of all mankind. Abinadi's words thrilled Alma, but also caused him to shudder inside.

"But behold, and fear, and tremble before God, for ye ought to tremble; for the Lord redeemeth none such that rebel against him and die in their sins. Salvation will not come to those who wilfully rebel against God."

Alma's eyes misted as he thought of commandments he had broken. He thought of Esther and Zoram. Would they be more pure than he? Would they be part of the first resurrection Abinadi had spoken of, and not he? The pain was almost too much to bear.

Abinadi stretched hands imploringly towards the priests. "The time shall come when all shall see the salvation of the Lord; when every nation, kindred, tongue, and people shall see eye to eye and shall confess before God that his judgments are just. Then shall the wicked be cast out. Remember, he that persists in his own carnal nature, and goes on in the ways of sin and rebellion against God, remains in his fallen state and the devil has all power over him. Therefore he is an enemy to God."

Another tremor went through Alma's body. He felt as if Abinadi spoke directly to him. Then Abinadi talked of a way to remove his guilt.

"The arms of mercy are extended towards all who have sinned. Remember that only in and through Christ can you be saved." Alma wrote as quickly as he could, attempting to get all of Abinadi's words. Abinadi spoke of the law of Moses being only a shadow of what would come. He spoke of the redemption which would come through the Christ, of mortal putting on immortality, and corruption putting on incorruption."

His sermon ended, "If they be good, to the resurrection of endless life and happiness; and if they be evil, to the resurrection of endless damnation."

Alma glanced at King Noah. The king apparently didn't comprehend anything that Abinadi was saying and was obviously becoming angrier with each sentence. He commanded,

"Guards, seize this imposter." He turned to the priests, an evil look in his eye. "You have heard him. He is guilty of inciting the people. You priests take him and put him to death."

Fully understanding the consequences of his action but knowing that he must now do what was right, Alma stood.

"Wait!"

King and priests turned to look at Alma.

"What is it?"

"My king and fellow priests. I have listened carefully during hours of interrogation. This man has not spoken anything we have not been taught before by our fathers and our sacred writings. I say we release him and let him depart in peace."

King Noah's eyes bulged. The cords in his neck distended as anger rose.

"You dare oppose me?" he shouted. "Away with you! Get out of this palace before I have you killed. You are a traitor to me and to your fellow priests."

Alma gathered his papers and fled, his fear prompting speed. He glanced back only once. The guards held Abinadi. Other priests stood by, colorful robes seeming out of place in the grayness of Alma's vision. He sweated, both from his exertion and from the fear that now had hold of him. What would happen to him and his family now that he had opposed the king?

Chapter 2

Escape From Nephi

"Alma! Alma!"

The shout's urgency made Alma hurry to the door. Helam brushed past, grabbed Alma and pulled him back inside.

"What is it, my friend?"

"It is your own foolish words, Alma, that's what it is," Helam replied grimly. "They have really got you into trouble this time. Noah is after your head and the priests are with him."

"Is it because I supported Abinadi?"

Helam spoke sarcastically. "You have taken this so-called prophet's side against king and all his priests. Is it any wonder the king is angry with you?"

"But I believe Abinadi. I think he is a prophet."

"He may well be," Helam said. "But that doesn't help your situation. The king's guards are on their way right now to arrest you. Noah has called for your death."

Alma's only reaction was a sharp intake of breath. Would his uncle really have him killed? He nodded grimly in the affirmative.

He asked, "What shall I do?"

Helam said, "If I were in your sandals, I would leave the City of Nephi as quickly as possible. I would find someplace to hide until the king forgot me."

"But where?"

Impatiently, Helam answered. "It doesn't matter. Just go."

"But what of Esther, and Zoram, and my books and papers?"

"We'll get them to you. Now go before it's too late! Quickly. Out through the garden. After dark I will meet you at the Shilom tower. Go!"

"But Esther . . . ?"

"I'll take care of Esther." Helam pushed him out into the garden, looked around cautiously, then sneaked out himself.

* * *

Esther, out walking with young Zoram, hoped Alma would be home. Life seemed much more pleasant when he was there. She entered the house and called.

"Alma."

No response. Disappointed, she began taking off her scarf.

Pounding came at the door. "Open up in the name of the king!"

She hurried to the door. Four guards armed with long spears stood there. She gasped. Unconsciously her hand went to her mouth. Her throat constricted in fear.

"We have come for your husband. Where is he?" The voice was gruff and unfriendly.

Unable to speak, she shook her head. Finally she said, "He isn't here. He is at the court of the king."

The officer roughly pushed her aside, forcing his way in. The other guards followed. Esther ran to where little Zoram was playing on the floor. She picked him up and held him protectively to her. Wild thoughts went through her mind. Where is Alma? What has he done? Why has the king sent guards for him? Oh, he must be in trouble.

After a fruitless search the guards returned. The leader, spear in hand, stopped before Esther. Leaning on the heavy spear, he growled, "When your husband returns, he is to report to the king's palace."

Helplessly Esther stood with Zoram in her arms while the guard's eyes roved from her feet back to her head. She felt stripped to the skin before his ruthless gaze.

He smiled mirthlessly. "I may see you later." Then he added, "After we have taken care of your husband." He motioned with his head and the guards tramped out, leaving the door open.

Esther stepped quickly to the door, noticing the guards still talking in the street. The leader and one other guard walked back towards the palace. Two guards remained before her home. She closed the door and leaned against it, clutching her baby tightly to her. He struggled to get down, and she slowly sank to the floor with Zoram still in her arms.

She whispered, "Oh, my husband, I don't know what you have done, but please come back to me. I need you. Don't let them hurt you."

Little Zoram looked at her with wide eyes, pulled free, and scampered into his bedroom, the cubiculum.

There was a tapping on the garden gate. She sat, her back against the front door, almost afraid to move. Who could it be? Perhaps it is Alma! She stood and hurried through the garden.

It was Alma's friend, Helam. He took her hands in his and whispered, "I saw the guards out front." "What is it? What has happened to Alma?"

Gently Helam led her into the house. He sat her at the table and then sat next to her.

Still holding her hands, he said, "Alma is all right. He is in trouble for defending Abinadi and had to flee from the king."

Esther audibly sucked in her breath, then put her hand over her mouth. Her eyes were large with fright.

Helam squeezed her hands, then continued. "I have arranged a place to meet him tonight. He is concerned about you, so we must sneak you out of the city."

"But . . . "

He shook his head. "There is no time for discussion. Pack what things Alma will need in bags that you and I can carry. He specifically asked for his scrolls and some parchment on which to write."

"What about his clothes and food and . . . ?"

Helam seemed impatient. "You can pack some clothes, but there is enough food available in the forest. Just hurry. We don't have much time."

"My son, Zoram. We cannot take him with us."

Helam frowned. "Your parents. Do they live near here?"

"Near the north wall in the city's older part."

"Good. We'll drop Zoram there. They can take care of him until we return."

Helam stopped at the gate, then returned. "If the guards ask, tell them you are going to stay with your parents until Alma returns."

"What about you?"

"I'll meet you after dark in the back street behind their house."

He hurried out.

Esther put Alma's robe and extra sandals in a goatskin bag, then slipped in some of Alma's favorite breads. She put a loaf to her nose and smelled it before she put the bread in the bag. Alma always enjoyed the smell of fresh-baked bread. She packed a separate bag of clothes for little Zoram.

Dusk came quickly in the valley. Esther lighted a candle, then gathered up Alma's scrolls, brushes, and a length of bark paper. Darkness had fallen by the time she stepped outside, her bundle in one arm and leading little Zoram with the other. She walked with a confidence she didn't feel. Carefully shutting the gate behind her, she turned up the back street towards her parent's home. Her footsteps seemed to echo loudly against the walls; her heart thumped rapidly in her chest.

Her skin prickled when someone stepped out of the darkness to join her. She breathed a sigh of relief when she saw it was Helam. Without a word Helam scooped up Zoram and led them up a dark side street. He walked so quickly that Esther almost had to run to keep up with him. She turned her head, listening, but could hear no pursuit.

Esther's parents seemed glad to see them. Esther could see they were curious about what had happened, but she was grateful they didn't ask any questions. They took Zoram graciously and she quickly slipped back outside and joined Helam.

The guards at the city gate, apparently recognizing Helam, waved them through. That's one advantage of being a homebody, Esther thought. The guards don't know that I am Alma's wife. Once outside the walls she breathed easier.

The night was dark and Esther could not see where she was going. She blindly followed Helam. As she walked, to avoid worrying, she thought of Helam, her husband's friend. He was a priest, but older than Alma. His dark hair was streaked with gray. He was indistinct in the dark, but Esther remembered his strong dimpled chin, his wide-set hazel eyes. He had kept his body strong and agile, and she wished now that he would slow down just a little bit.

The trail wound through the forest. Tree branches constantly slapped against her. Several times she tripped over rocks or tree roots. Once she banged her knee, making walking painful. She had never been out in the forest in the dark and each sound brought her heart to her throat. Her legs were tired and her breath came in ragged gasps. They had been toiling uphill for almost an hour when Esther felt the ground level off under her feet. She bumped into Helam as he suddenly stopped.

Shilom's tower stood starkly before her, dark against the sky. She panted for breath as she looked curiously at the tower. Noah had built the tower in the center of a beautiful meadow. Alma's father had told her that several hundred years before—before they abandoned the City of Nephi and moved to the Land of Zarahemla—the meadow had been a popular resort among the descendants of Nephi. Noah had taxed the people heavily to build the tower where he could consort with his concubines. Esther had heard how Noah often drank himself into a stupor here in this tower.

As soon as she caught her breath, Helam started walking again. Esther followed as they skirted the forest's edge. She was glad that here in the open the starlight was bright enough for her to see her way.

Helam cupped his hands and gave a strange bird cry. From the forest ahead came an answer. They resumed their journey when suddenly before them a form materialized out of the darkness.

"Friend, you kept your word."

"Of course, and I brought someone to see you."

"Esther?" Alma's voice broke with gladness.

She stepped forward and threw her arms around Alma's neck. They embraced for a long moment, then Alma found her lips and kissed her. He slipped his arm around her waist and they turned to Helam. Esther brushed a wisp of damp hair off her lightly-perspiring face.

"Where is Zoram?" Alma asked.

"We left him with Esther's parents," Helam answered before Esther could respond.

"What is the situation in Noah's court?"

"Not good. Right after you left, the king had his guards take Abinadi to the prison for execution."

"Helam, I am convinced that Abinadi is a prophet of God. Is there anything we can do to save him?"

"I, too, have begun to believe that he speaks the truth," Helam admitted. Shaking his head sadly, he said, "But there is nothing we can do. He is in prison and is heavily guarded." He paused, then continued with fervor, "But right now I am more concerned about you. Alma, what are you going to do? Where will you stay?"

Esther looked into her husband's face. She felt the same concerns.

Alma squeezed her. "I have considered that. In the forest near here, there is a cave where I will keep dry. I feel that I must stay close to the city, at least until we see that nothing more can be done for Abinadi."

"I think after a few days the king will lose interest in you," Helam said. Then he added sarcastically, "He is too busy eating, drinking and philandering with all his concubines to be concerned about some errant priest."

"What of Esther and my son? Are they in any danger by staying in the city?"

Helam shrugged. "There is no telling what our mighty king will do." He paused for thought. "However, just to make sure, the best course might be to have them temporarily move in with Esther's parents. No place will be completely safe from Noah's anger, but he may not act against so many."

Esther reacted strongly. "No. I will live in my own home. Now that I know Alma is safe, I can take care of myself."

She saw the flash of Alma's teeth as he smiled in the darkness. "Solomon was right when he said 'a virtuous wife is a crown to her husband,' " he said. "And especially a virtuous wife who is not only beautiful but strong-willed."

Esther looked up to see if he was teasing before she asked, "Will you be able to return to the city at a later time?" "I don't know. All depends on King Noah. I will remain here in hiding until I am sure there is no danger."

"Then I will join you in the forest. We can live together in your cave."

He squeezed her gently. "That may be necessary later. Right now we must think of our son. He is better off in the city. Later . . . ." He left the thought unsaid.

"What will you do?"

"The first thing I want to do is write Abinadi's words. I have a feeling the Lord wants them recorded and preserved as a testimony against the people's wickedness."

After more minutes of visiting, Helam spoke. "We must get back to the city. We don't want the guards to get suspicious. Three nights from now we will meet you again."

"I will meet you outside the city wall where the east trail crosses the stream."

"Good." Helam seemed anxious to be off.

Esther turned her face up to Alma's. He pulled her to him, and they kissed for a long moment. He released her with a sigh.

Tears dimmed her vision, but she turned and blindly followed Helam as he started back down the trail.

* * *

Three days passed quickly. Helam and Esther found Alma right where he said he would be.

After initial greetings, Alma asked Helam. "What of Abinadi?"

Helam paused before answering. Turning away from them he spoke with sadness. "Abinadi was executed this morning by the priests."

Alma gasped. "Executed?"

"Yes. He died the fiery death."

Alma sat down, his head in his hands. Esther sat beside him, rubbing his back as if he were a child to be comforted.

He looked up with anguished eyes. "Tell me. Did he say anything before he died?"

Helam choked up and for a moment couldn't talk. He swallowed several times to control his emotion, then, he quietly narrated Abinadi's last days to Alma and Esther.

* * *

Abinadi, his robe ragged and dirty from his stay in the dungeon, stood again before Noah and his priests. Even in filth and chains he presented a dignified appearance. He gazed calmly at his accusers.

The king, uncomfortable before his stare, began, "Abinadi, we have found you guilty of heresy. You said that God himself will come and live on the earth. Unless you recall these and all the other evil words which you have spoken against my people, you will die."

Speaking so quietly that Noah had to lean forward and strain to hear, Abinadi said, "I will not recall my words. They are true; you know they are true. It was God's purpose that I fall into your hands so I could witness against you. God's purpose will be fulfilled even if you kill me, for then my innocent blood will forever be on your hands."

Noah, visibly shaken, paled. Sweat glistened on his forehead and formed rivulets down his cheeks. He ran a fleshy palm across his face then looked for support to the priests sitting before him.

He looked back at Abinadi. "If you will just take back the evil words you have spoken against us, we can let you go," he said almost pleadingly.

Abinadi was silent.

Again Noah looked at his priests. He was wavering.

Amulon stood, casting a withering glance at the ragged man before him. "This man deserves to die. He has reviled the king, condemned our people, and given false prophesies. I say we execute this heretic now. Enough with words."

"Aye," came the shouted chorus from the priests. "Kill him." Only Helam was silent.

"Aye," Noah nodded, as color returned to his face. "He shall die. Away with him!"

The priests surged around Abinadi, almost carrying him as they pushed into the square before the palace. The place of execution, a stout pine pole buried part-way in the ground, had already been prepared. Dry and pitchy pine wood was heaped around the pole. Abinadi was chained securely to the pole.

Amulon himself applied the torch. Wisps of smoke curled upwards from twigs and branches. Then, as fire caught hold, flames swirled around Abinadi's bare feet and legs. He winced as the first burning pain hit him. Then he shut his eyes, steeling himself against pain, offering a prayer that he might endure. The smell of scorched flesh filled the square. Abinadi writhed in agony. Opening his eyes, he cried. "King Noah, even as you have done unto me, your seed shall make many suffer the pains of death by fire. Because of your wickedness you shall be afflicted with disease. You and your people shall be smitten and shall be driven and scattered to and fro, even as a wild flock is driven by wild and ferocious beasts."

His hair caught fire. Almost unconscious, he gritted his teeth against the increasing pain. Through reddened eyes he looked directly at Noah and moaned, "You shall be hunted and captured by your enemies. Then you shall suffer as I am suffering, even the pains of death by fire." His voice weakened. "Thus God executes vengeance upon those who destroy his people."

As the flames licked upwards on his body, he looked up to the heavens, "O God," he cried, "receive my soul." His head slumped forward.

* * *

Alma listened sadly as Helam recounted Abinadi's last words. He sat, elbows resting on his knees, face buried in his hands. He was silent, thinking of the wickedness of Noah and his priests. Then the tears flowed. He was one of them. He was just as wicked as they. Because of him Abinadi had been captured in the first place. His tears were tears of anguish and remorse.

Esther pulled his head against her bosom, her hands gently stroking his back. His sobs subsided. Then he looked up with tear-reddened eyes. A new resolve showed in the set of his jaw.

"We must save as many of the people as we can from the consequences which Abinadi has predicted." He stood and faced the city. "Repentance must begin with me. I must have time to consider all I have done that is wrong in the sight of God." He turned to Esther, his hands on her shoulders. "Please leave me alone now. I will come by night to our house."

* * *

Alma couldn't sleep. Clear weather permitted him to make his bed out of the cave under the stars. He lay there staring up into the heavens, listening to the night sounds. He could not get the words of Abinadi out of his mind: *Wo be unto this people. Except they repent I will visit them in mine anger.*

When morning finally arrived, he carefully unrolled the scripture scrolls his father had given him so many years before. He read from the beginning of Nephi's record, marveling at the great faith of his forebear.

The words of his father came to him. "You are a descendant of Nephi. He established this city hundreds of years ago when he fled from the wickedness of his brothers."

He thrilled at Jacob's writings, then trembled in anguish of spirit when he read, "And he commanded all men that they must repent, and be baptized in his name, having perfect faith in the Holy one of Israel, or they cannot be saved in the kingdom of God.

"And if they will not repent and believe in his name, and be baptized in his name, and endure to the end, they must be damned; for the Lord God, the Holy One of Israel, has spoken it.

"Wo unto him who has the law given, yea, that has all the commandments of God, and that transgresseth them, and that wasteth the days of his probation, for awful is his state."

Alma's body was wet with sweat. He shivered involuntarily.

"Why? Why?" he cried aloud. "Here I have had these scriptures for years and have not read them. Why haven't I taken time to study and ponder them? Why didn't I follow my father's counsel?"

He recalled his father's words. "Search the scriptures. When you pray, the Lord will answer your prayers through the scriptures. How can you expect an answer from Him if you are not reading His word?"

His agony was real as he reviewed the wasted life he had led. Now he realized that having the scriptures available to him and not reading them was worse than not being able to read. He buried his head in his hands and sobbed aloud. And as for praying . . . ?

He reread the last passage. "Wo unto him who has the commandments and transgresseth them . . . awful is his state!"

He knelt. "Oh, God, please forgive me of my sins—especially the sin of complacency." He prayed continuously for several hours. Realizing he was weak and hadn't eaten for more than a day, he started to get up and find something to eat. Something made him hesitate.

Then he recalled more of his father's words. "When problems beset you, use fasting and prayer for your answers." Fasting! Perhaps that was the answer.

He hadn't thought of fasting for many years. King Noah's philosophy had been: "Indulge yourself. It's your life. Live to the fullest."

The thought of Noah's hedonistic philosophy triggered a memory. He remembered the day his father came home the last time from Noah's court. At that time the experience had not meant anything to him. His father had looked more tired and discouraged than Alma had ever seen him.

"King Noah has released me," Abimolam had told him. "He is staffing his court with new priests." He had paused reflectively. "He feels we are too old, with old ideas and old values."

Alma remembered how his father had accented each of the last words. Then shamefully, he remembered that secretly he had agreed with Noah.

"Old values?" He had asked his father, mainly just to make conversation.

Abimolam had shaken his head. "Yes. He has little concern for values of honesty and fidelity." A pained look had come into his eyes. "Noah is planning to find younger priests who will allow him to live a depraved life without having to feel guilty—priests who will justify his actions."

Thinking of his father's words, Alma bowed his head sorrowfully. "And I was one of those priests," he said aloud.

Kneeling once more, he offered a prayer that his fast might be fruitful. He read the scriptures until the sun faded behind the western hills, leaving the forest dark and brooding. Reading now impossible, he carefully carried the scrolls into the cave.

The night was clear with a high thin moon, and all heaven seemed filled with stars. Soft evergreen trees swayed gently above him, outlined black against the starry sky. He lay awake until the moon finally sank behind the hills. Night became pitch black, softened only by the pale light of many stars. Alma finally dozed.

Huge drops of rain hitting his face awakened him. He jumped up and blundered to his cave in the dark. He sat at the cave's mouth, blanket draped over his hunched shoulders. From there he watched as fingers of lightning danced around the sky. As dawn slowly brightened the east, he noticed that the lightning and thunder had stopped. Wind had also died to a quiet breeze, but rain drummed steadily against the ground. He was so depressed, and rain didn't help.

All day he sat, leaving the cave only for necessary functions. His mind was a turmoil: thoughts of what he had done; of what he had not done; of things he had heard his father speak; of words he had read; and especially of the sayings of Abinadi. Waves of remorse overcame him, causing him to kneel many times to pour out his soul to God. His many sins passed before him, and he shook his head in anguish. How could he have been so foolish? He had been given all the knowledge of the Gospel by his father. Why hadn't he followed those teachings?

He remembered guiltily how as a child he had asked his father about prayer. Abimolam had taken him on his lap; told him prayer was a way of talking to God and that he should address God as his father and his friend. His guilt feelings arose from the fact that all during his years as a priest, he had never once approached God in prayer.

Other things his father had told him came to mind: find a quiet place where you can be alone. "Then as you pray," he had said, "control your thoughts. Don't let them wander. As you talk to God, tell Him things you really want to tell Him. Confide in Him. Ask Him for forgiveness. Plead with Him. Thank Him. Express your love for Him. Then listen for His answer."

Alma remembered he had asked his father what God sounded like.

Abimolam had answered, "Few people hear God's answer with their ears. Most answers from the Lord are felt in our heart as a warm, comfortable feeling. Sometimes they may come as a voice in our mind."

Alma moaned aloud. "Oh, why haven't I been praying for these many years?" Then another thought came to him. "Will God even listen to me now, after neglecting to pray for years, and after all the things I have done? Will he turn a deaf ear to my pleading?"

Into his mind came words Abinadi had spoken, words predicting that a Savior would come to earth. Alma picked up a scroll on which he had written Abinadi's words.

"Thus God breaks the bands of death, having gained victory over death; giving the son power to make intercession for the children of men. Having ascended into heaven, having the bowels of mercy; being filled with compassion towards the children of men. He will take upon himself their iniquity and their transgressions, having redeemed them, and satisfied the demands of justice.

"All those who have hearkened unto the words of the prophets and believed that the Lord would redeem his people, and have looked forward to that day for a remission of their sins, I say unto you, that these are his seed. These are they whose sins he has borne; these are they for whom he has died, to redeem them from their transgressions."

Could it be? Could God be so merciful as to take upon Himself my sins? The thought was overpowering. Once again he prayed, this time pleading with the Lord. "Dear God, even the Jesus Christ which Abinadi said would come to earth, please hear my prayers. Please heal the anguish of my heart. Forgive me of my sins."

After what seemed an hour, Alma stood and stretched. His body ached from being in a cramped position. He stepped out of the cave to stretch his legs. He looked up at the blue sky, clear now except for a few clouds. Voluptuous sun wallowed low on the horizon, painting undersides of clouds a tawny orange.

Returning to the cave, he continued his prayer. Hunger gnawed at his stomach; his throat was raw; his mind a turmoil of self-deprecating thoughts. He felt anguish and hunger of spirit he had never felt before.

Exhausted, he fell asleep, prayers still unanswered. He awoke in a sweat. Once again his dreams were of Abinadi. He saw the straining and emaciated body of the prophet illuminated by flames which rose around him. He heard Abinadi's cries of denunciation of Noah and his priests, prophesying their destruction.

Morning found him weak and unsure that he could last through the day. He walked to the stream and sat on the bank. Dropping pebbles in the water, he watched the spreading of the ripples.

His reverie was interrupted by voices. He listened carefully. Who could it be? He remained motionless, his heart seeming to splinter his ribs with furious pounding. He had to get back to the cave. But how? He crawled to a large tree, keeping its trunk between him and the direction of the voices.

"This is a hopeless task."

"Yes, finding a lone man in this forest is almost like getting an extra gold senine of wages out of the king."

"Ha!"

"And if it weren't already bad enough, yesterday's rain wiped out any possible tracks."

Alma sucked in his breath. What of tracks he had made from the cave today? He prayed, Father, please take them away from here. Let them not find me until I have completed Thy work.

He pressed himself against the tree. They were so close. I cannot be found now, he thought. I have too much to do. He listened as the guards discussed other things. He waited there, hardly daring to breathe. Finally, the voices began to fade. "Well, at least we can report we searched this sector of woods."

"Nothing here but squirrels."

Alma let out his breath in a sigh of relief. The Lord was with him. Carefully keeping to cover, he returned to the cave. There he again dropped to his knees. What more could he say without being repetitious?

"Father, I want to dedicate my life to thy service. I turn my life over to Thee. Use me as Thou desirest. Permit me to teach the words of Thy Son, Jesus Christ, who will come to earth. Let me be like ripples in the brook—expanding Thy influence and scattering Thy word to all who will listen."

Suddenly a feeling of calmness came upon him. As this peace permeated his being, a voice spoke to his consciousness.

"Alma, my son, thy sins are forgiven thee."

He jumped and looked around. He had heard a voice. Was he imagining? Had the Lord really spoken to his mind? Or in his travail, had his mind just played tricks on him? He continued praying.

Again the voice came to him, "Alma, my son, do not doubt. Your repentance is acceptable to me. I have a work for you. Go and preach to this people. Their sins are as scarlet before me. Be as Abinadi. Call the people to repentance and baptize them. As long as you are humble and serve me, my spirit will be with you."

His heart sang within him. His sins were forgiven! He felt renewed and clean. The joyous feeling within him was greater than anything he had ever experienced. He had never felt such a warmth. He walked back to the nearby stream, bathed thoroughly and put on a clean robe.

The time had come. He was ready to serve as a true priest of the Lord God. From his bag he pulled a dried fish wrapped in leaves. As he ate he felt strength flowing back into his body. The sun rose high in the sky, bringing a new day.

"I, too, am ready to start a new day," he said aloud. He squared his broad shoulders. "The Lord has given me a fresh start."

Chapter 3

The Waters of Mormon

Alma walked boldly into the city, directly to his father's home. Abimolam seemed overjoyed to see him.

"Alma, my son, I have worried about you."

"There is no longer any cause to worry, father."

"But the king's guards were here. Why are they seeking you? What have you done? Where have you been?"

"One question at a time, father." Alma chuckled. He spoke gently. "First, the reason the king seeks me is that I defended Abinadi, the prophet, before him. Father, I know that Abinadi is truly a prophet."

He took his father's hands in his. "Father, I am converted. I have been in the forest pleading with the Lord for forgiveness." He added softly, "And the Lord has spoken to me."

As Alma spoke, Abimolam sank to his knees, still holding Alma's hands. Tears ran freely down his wrinkled cheeks.

Alma helped his father to a bench, then sat down beside him. "Father, the Lord instructed me to teach and baptize the people. With your help, the scriptures, and the words of Abinadi, I will be able to teach. But baptize? I am not sure what to do. Years have passed since baptisms were permitted in the land."

"My son, trust the Lord. He will guide you. Know that you are operating with His authority. While you were yet a youth I ordained you to the priesthood of God."

"But I have not honored the priesthood. How can I be sure I still have it?"

Abimolam smiled. "Your repentance has given you back the rights of the priesthood. The Lord will not let you down. Trust Him."

Alma sighed with relief. "Father, I desire one other favor of you."

The grayed head bowed in apparent gratitude. "Many years have passed since you asked me for anything."

Alma laid a hand on his father's bony knee. "Father, I ask your forgiveness for my neglect. I thought I was happy doing the bidding of the king. Now I know that it was not true happiness. True happiness would have been staying true to my beliefs—true to what you taught me." He ducked his head and composed his thoughts. "Father, I desire of you a blessing."

Tears welled in the old man's eyes, then overflowed unheeded. He wiped his nose and cleared his throat. For a moment he couldn't speak. Then he rose and shuffled around behind the chair upon which Alma was sitting. He laid his hands on his son's head and began his blessing.

Alma concentrated hard on the words. He felt the spirit and strength of his father as he listened.

"Honor your priesthood. It is the power of God unto salvation. Teach the people repentance and the plan of redemption. Be always true to the covenants which you will make with the Lord and He will always bless you."

When his father was through, Alma stood and hugged him.

His father said, "Oh, how I wish that your mother were here. She would be so happy."

"Father, I believe that mother is here."

* * *

"Come now," Zephany said. "It is difficult for me to comprehend that this is the priest of Noah speaking of repentance."

Alma smiled understandingly at the irony in Zephany's words. "I know what you are thinking, my friend, but I speak truth. I have listened to a prophet speak and the Lord has witnessed that his words were true. Now I feel it is extremely important that I share those words with my friends."

"But if what you say is correct, then this entire people is in danger of damnation!"

Alma nodded soberly. "Zephany, that is why I am telling you and other friends about Abinadi's prophecies. There is still time. We must create a cadre of believers. Then that cadre can help the entire people to see the truth."

"What does King Noah say about all of this?"

A shrug was Alma's only reply. He leaned closer to Zephany. "As a lawyer, you have been a city leader. I encourage you to think carefully about what I have said."

He gripped Zephany's arm, stood, and strode out the door, leaving Zephany in apparent deep thought.

* * *

In the next few weeks Alma called on scores of people, talking with them as he had Zephany, leaving his message of repentance and salvation. He found that many people had heard Abinadi speak and were receptive to his words. To help people understand the urgency of his message, he often quoted from the sermon Abinadi gave before Noah's priestly court: "You ought to fear and tremble before God, for the Lord redeems none that rebel against Him and die in their sins. Therefore, shouldn't you tremble? Salvation will not come to those who rebel against God."

As he visited with his friend, Amarta, a banging came at the door.

"Noah's soldiers!" Amarta whispered. "They have been seeking you for days."

Alma glanced at Amarta, an imploring look in his eyes. Amarta nodded and motioned. Alma hurried after him, quickly climbing down into the serdab, a root cellar, below the rock floor. Amarta replaced the floorstone and threw a rug over it as the pounding became more insistent.

The cellar room was dank, dark, and close. Alma tried to breathe calmly as he listened to thuds of heavy feet and sounds of angry voices over his head. There were scuffling sounds and then silence. There were no other sounds for some time, then he heard the stone rasping as Amarta lifted it once more. The rush of fresh air and light of day gave blessed relief.

He looked at Armata. There was a cut on his friend's cheek and one eye was beginning to swell and blacken. Amarta breathed deeply and nodded his head. "That was too close, my friend. The captain of the guard said someone informed him they saw you enter my home. Now I am also under suspicion."

Alma climbed out and stood by his friend. He put his hand on his shoulder. "Are you all right?"

Amarta smiled with one side of his mouth. "The beatings of Noah's guards will not deter me from joining with you."

"Then you are with me?"

"Of course. You have convinced me. What do we do now that Noah has found out you are preaching to the people?"

"One thing I do know. It is too dangerous to remain in the City of Nephi. I must find a retreat: some place where our people can gather; a place where they won't be disturbed by Noah or his soldiers." A dreamy look came into his eyes. "A place where we can worship our God and can live in peace and harmony."

"I suppose you know that wherever you go there will be risk to you and your followers."

Alma smiled. "I've learned an important lesson during the past few weeks. Everything we do has some risk in it. The only security we have is what is within us, and the risk of doing nothing is the worst risk of all."

Amarta studied the young man before him. "How long has it been since you were to the Waters of Mormon?"

Alma looked at Amarta quizzically. "Waters of Mormon? Isn't that where there are so many wild and ferocious animals? No one has dared go there . . . " A look of understanding came into his eyes. He nodded. "The Waters of Mormon may be the perfect place." He became more excited as he talked. "Why, there's a lake for baptizing, a forest to hide in, many trees bearing fruit and nuts."

Amarta smiled.

"But what of animals?"

"Someone was frightened there many years ago. Rumors spread and now no one goes there. The place is several day's walk from the city. There you will find the isolation you desire."

Alma put his arms around his friend. "Thank you. I shall leave the city tonight and travel there tomorrow. I have not been to the Land of Mormon since I was a child and will need to scout it out. If it is a good place for us to gather, I will send word to you."

After dark, Alma, disguised as a woodsman, slipped out of the city and returned to his cave to sleep. When morning came, he packed the few things he would need and started westward. As he passed near the city he stayed close to the forest, avoiding contact with people. When the sun was at its highest point, he stopped for lunch. He dozed for a few minutes in the shade of a ceiba tree, then again made his way westward, walking tirelessly as the land sloped upward. Alma camped overnight near a small stream. He fell asleep listening to the tinkling of water as it cascaded over rocks.

Morning found him toiling upward through thick forests as the ground rose more steeply. Alma remembered there were towering cone-shaped volcanoes ringing the lake known as the Waters of Mormon. He breathed a sigh of relief when he saw them thrusting their peaks into the sky.

Night came before he reached the lake. The moon had finished its first quarter and gave enough radiance for him to continue. He walked until the perfect cone-shaped volcanoes blotted out the entire sky to the west. He found a place to sleep where he could see moonlight shining faintly on water. He knew he was at the Waters of Mormon. As he knelt and prayed, he asked the Lord to affirm to him that this was the place for gathering his people. When his prayer was finished, a feeling of calmness and peace filled his being. He knew it was the right place.

Morning opened up for him a marvelous sight. The valley fell away sharply before him. In the center of the valley was a beautiful emerald-green lake. Ringing the lake on the west were three perfectly formed volcanic cones. Lush forests grew to the water's edge. The lake was a huge one. He mentally measured it with his eye, estimating that to paddle across it would take most of a day. Since the lake was practically surrounded by mountains, he suspected there was no outlet. The lake looked extremely deep, with water clear as crystal.

Alma recalled that the lake was near the border of the Land of Nephi-Lehi. The distance, along with the rumors about the presence of fierce animals, would give his people privacy they desired. The area was the perfect meeting place. He filled his lungs with the mountain air, enjoying the pine and sage smell. Alma had been reared in the city. Now as he looked around him at the great beauty of mountains, lakes and forests he wished he had spent more time out of the city, enjoying the beauties of nature.

After making sure no one lived near the lake, he started his return journey. All the way he mentally rehearsed plans for helping people to leave the city. He was glad many of those who would follow him lived outside the walls. First ones to leave would have to be Esther and Zoram, his father, Abimolam, and Helam's family.

After two days of walking, Alma arrived again at the City of Nephi. He waited until dark and took no chances by going to one of the city gates, but climbed over the wall near his in-laws' home. Esther had decided to stay with her parents, for which he was glad. Waiting until the house was dark, he rapped softly on the wall. He didn't hear a sound, but suddenly Esther stood beside him at the door. Wrapping his arms tenderly around her, he kissed her. It was a kiss of longing and loneliness.

"Esther, my love," he said. "Get things that you and Zoram will need. Join me outside the east gate in the morning when the sun is at its first position." He held her at arm's length. "I must leave now and warn others."

"Must you leave so soon?" she pleaded.

"The sooner I leave, the sooner we can be together."

"Stay just a few minutes."

"No, dearest. I want very much to stay, but I must see all of the others before dawn lights the sky."

Esther drew him close and kissed him again.

"You make it very hard to leave," he said, holding her soft lithe body tightly against him. Another long kiss and he released her.

She wrapped her fingers in the hair of his chest and laughed teasingly. He turned her towards the door, and with his open hand spatted her behind. She was still laughing quietly as she went inside.

"I love you," he whispered, as she quietly closed the door behind her.

He hurried away. The night would be busy. He kept to shadows as he made a circuit of the city. By the time Venus was setting in the east, he had contacted his father, Helam, Zephany, Amarta, and several other friends who had embraced the Gospel. To all he gave similar instructions.

"Pass the word to those who have listened. Take your own families and leave the city. Meet at the Waters of Mormon."

Climbing the wall once again, he made his way to his cave. He was tired, but very happy. Let Noah try to stop them now!

* * *

Passing lava promontories and low mountains, Alma led Esther, Zoram and Abimolam towards the lake. Ahead of them they herded Abimolam's small flock of goats. A new member of the family also accompanied them, against Alma's wishes. Alma looked often at the short-legged ball of fur that scampered around Zoram's feet. Esther's parents had given Zoram a puppy, brown and white and all tongue. Alma had not wanted to bring the puppy but Esther had prevailed.

They traveled slowly, respecting Abimolam's age, even though Alma thought that since his conversion Abimolam looked at least ten years younger.

They barely had time to set up their tent in the place Alma had selected before it grew dark. Alma was glad the tent had a partition. He had Zoram and the puppy sleep in the front with his father, and he and Esther took the back section. From the front of the tent they soon heard the whimpering of the puppy, punctuated by the snores of Abimolam. The night outside was rent by territorial bickering of parrots, screams of tree frogs and distant roars of wild animals. Esther huddled close to Alma. He smiled in the dark.

He pulled her to him and kissed her tenderly. She trembled in his arms and again his lips found hers in sweet union. With a soft little cry of delight, she returned his kiss. Discovering each other anew, neither Alma nor Esther heard the mournful crying of the jaguar off in the forest.

With Esther cuddled into the curve of his arm, Alma breathed in the night air and the sweetness of her scent. He listened to her deep regular breathing and knew that she was asleep. He lay awake for awhile, thinking: so now we start a new phase of our lives.

The second day passed quickly as Alma and his family toiled steadily upwards. They slowed down as the slope steepened. Alma could tell that Abimolam was tired. They were all relieved when they finally made camp. Alma, anxious to observe Esther's response, had brought them to his previous campsite.

Next morning they awakened to the splendor of a brilliant sunrise. From their camp they looked down on the Waters of Mormon. The lake was incredibly beautiful. In the clear sparkling sunlight of spring morning it gleamed and glittered like the fairest of emeralds. As they watched, the smooth surface was ruffled by errant gusts of wind which deepened the emerald color to an almost translucent aquamarine. When it calmed, a reflected mirror-image of volcanic cones was inverted on the lake's emerald mirror.

Esther seemed enthralled. "It is so beautiful."

Alma squeezed her. "I don't know how long we will be here, but for now, this shall be our home."

By evening, Helam and a large group of converts arrived. Alma respected Helam's leadership ability, so he gave him responsibility for setting up camp. Alma walked with him through the area, listening as Helam gave instructions for setting up tents and constructing brush shelters in the forest where they couldn't be seen. After shelters were erected, Helam supervised the men as they dug latrines and set up cooking areas. Areas were designated for pasturing the flocks which the people had brought with them. The lake was to be used for bathing. Drinking water and water for cooking would come from streams emptying into the lake.

Alma had instructed people to leave the city by twos and threes, pretending to go to tend their flocks or to gather firewood. There were many reasons to be away from the city, so he left their departure to their imagination. Now, here they were—several hundred people with flocks of sheep and goats. He looked over people as they arrived. They were of all ages but it seemed that the elderly were more prominent. I guess that is only logical, he thought. They are like my father—brought up during King Zeniff's reign when righteousness was in favor.

As he watched people setting up camp, Alma humbly petitioned the Lord for strength and wisdom to lead. He felt great responsibility.

He called a meeting on an open hillside near the lake. His heart filled with joy as he looked over the congregation. Seated in front were his wife and son. On one side were his friends, Helam and his wife, Annah. On the other sat his father, Abimolam, and Esther's parents. Other friends nodded or waved as he stood before them.

"My friends," he began. "Each of you has left the security of the city to become part of this congregation. I believe this will be one of the most important decisions of your life. Thank you for having the courage to make that decision.

"My heart is full as I look at your faces. Some of you have sacrificed your families, your friends, your wealth or position in order to be here. The Lord has promised that He will bless you. Know that in His eternal plan, He has promised that He will restore all things to you for any losses which you might suffer here.

"Each has prepared for this moment. Today I ask you to make another decision." He turned and pointed to the lake. "Before you are the Waters of Mormon. If we are truly to be of one heart and one mind, we must now make the decision to be baptized."

Zebulon stood. Alma nodded for him to ask his question.

"I remember being told as a child about baptism. I have even read of our forefathers being baptized. Alma, we are as children. I am not sure we know enough about baptism to make that decision."

Alma was unsure how to respond. If truth were known, he was having similar feelings. He caught his father's eye. Abimolam winked.

"My friends, Zebulon's point is well-taken. None of us has been schooled, as yet, in the ordinances. My father, Abimolam, was a priest under righteous King Zeniff. Baptism was an important part of his duties. I will let him explain."

Alma helped his father to his feet. Abimolam stood with dignity before the congregation. As he spoke, his countenance shone.

"Baptism," he began, "cleanses us from guilt we might be feeling for things we have done. Baptism is a symbol to the Lord of our repentance and provides a way for the remission of our sins. When you come forth from the water, if you have repented of your sins, they are completely washed away. You are then admitted to the Lord's kingdom.

"Baptism should be a reminder of the death, burial and resurrection of the Savior who will come. In baptism, we are buried in the water in the likeness of Christ's burial in the tomb. We come forth from the water in likeness of His resurrection. Our baptism should always be a personal reminder of Christ's victory over death and His assurance that we will rise again."

He sat down. Alma smiled at him, then continued speaking.

"When Abinadi stood before Noah's court, he quoted from writings of Isaiah concerning the suffering which father spoke of. Let me read to you from writings of the brass plates. Isaiah said, 'Surely he has borne our griefs, and carried our sorrows; . . . he was wounded for our transgressions, he was bruised for our iniquities; . . . with his stripes we are healed. All we, like sheep, have gone astray; we have turned every one to his own way; and the Lord hath laid on him the iniquities of us all . . . for the transgressions of my people was he stricken . . . he bore the sin of many, and made intercession for the transgressors.' "

Amalakiahah asked, "Do you mean that God, himself, shall bear our sins?"

"Please understand that I am learning just as you are," Alma answered humbly. "But God has whispered to my consciousness that Abinadi's words are true. Abinadi testified before Noah and the priests that God himself shall come down among the children of men to redeem his people; that as the Son of God, He shall be subject to death.

"Abinadi said after working many mighty miracles among the people He would be led as a sheep to be slain. But realize, Amalakiahah and all of you, that His death is not the important thing. Through His resurrection He will gain victory over death. Through Him, each of us, though we may die, will rise again.

"Now, the question for us is the same question Abinadi raised, 'Who shall be his seed?' Which of you is ready for baptism?"

A mighty shout went up from the congregation. Many, filled with the spirit, stood and clapped their hands.

Alma stretched out his arms and quieted the jubilant throng. "Through your acclamation, I know of your desire to become part of the fold of God and to be called His people. That is my desire, also. But realize that such a decision commits you to bear one another's burdens; you will mourn with those who mourn; comfort those who stand in need of comfort, and will stand as witnesses of God at all times, in all things, and in all places where you may be until your death. At that time, if you have kept your covenants, you will be redeemed of God and will be numbered with those of the first resurrection.

"If this is the desire of your hearts, then come forth and be baptized in the name of the Lord, as a witness before Him that you have entered into a covenant with Him to serve Him and keep His commandments. By doing this, He will pour out His spirit upon you."

Another shout went up. "This is our desire! This is the desire of our hearts."

Alma motioned for them to be seated, then turned and walked to the lake. A line of people quickly formed behind him. Alma turned. Helam stepped forward, reached out his hand and Alma took it. Together they walked into the water. When they were up to their waists, they stopped. The only sound was the yapping of Zoram's small dog and the cries of birds in the forest.

Alma bowed his head. "Lord, bless me that Thy Spirit may abide in me, that I may do this work with holiness of heart." He immediately felt power. Vibrant strength encompassed his entire body. He felt renewed and vitalized.

Holding Helam's hand, he raised his right hand, "Helam, having authority from the Almighty God, I baptize you as a testimony that you have entered into a covenant to serve Him all of your life. May His Spirit be poured out upon you, and may He grant unto you eternal life, through the redemption of Christ, whom He has prepared from the foundation of the world. In the name of the Father, and of the Son, and of the Holy Ghost, Amen."

He ducked into the water, pulling Helam under with him. When they came out he noticed how Helam's countenance shown with the Spirit. His own face burned and he felt that it must also be shining. Helam threw his arms around him, and they embraced.

His wife, Esther, was next. Gently he led her into the water, then with great love said, "My dear Esther, having been commissioned of Jesus Christ, I baptize you in the name of the Father, and of the Son, and of the Holy Ghost, Amen." As he pulled her forth from the water, he felt a closeness to his wife that he had never felt before. Unashamedly they embraced while smiling people waited.

One after another, people walked into the water to where Alma stood. By mid-morning everyone old enough had been baptized. Alma's arms were sore from the strain but he hardly felt them.

Alma and the last person baptized slowly walked out of the water. Helam laid his hand on Alma's arm.

"Thank you," he whispered. "Thank you for believing the words of Abinadi and for having courage to stand up for what you believed. Without that belief and courage none of us would be here, and I wouldn't be feeling the joy that I am feeling."

Alma, filled with the spirit, couldn't speak. He nodded as his eyes misted.

Helam showed him a piece of bark paper. "I kept track of baptisms for you," he said. "You baptized two hundred and three people today."

"Does that include me?"

"No."

"Then there were two hundred four." He took the paper, put his arm around Helam's shoulders, and walked to where people waited.

Once more he stood before his people. A new look showed in their eyes. Alma felt burning in his own bosom as the Spirit witnessed to him the rightness of what they had done. He hoped each person felt that burning.

"My dear brothers and sisters," he said. "Today we are reborn. By being baptized, we not only receive a remission of our sins, but we enter into a new covenant with the Lord that we will always remember Him and keep His commandments." He paused and looked lovingly over the congregation. "Today, we have become members of the Church of God."

* * *

"What do you mean you cannot find this apostate priest?" Noah shouted.

Gideon, captain of the guard, stood before the king. "Alma is not to be found, my king," he said.

"You shall all be whipped!"

The guards behind Gideon quavered.

"What of his wife and child?" Amulon, the chief priest, asked.

"They are gone from the city, also," replied Gideon.

"And his father, Abimolam?"

"Also gone."

"And no one seems to know where they have gone?" fumed the king.

"No one, your majesty."

Amulon walked over and whispered into the king's ear. Noah looked up at Gideon, a frown on his face. "Amulon tells me that there has been an exodus from the city."

"Yes, my king. Several hundred people have left." Gideon added, "We detained three families with their herd of goats."

"And where are they now?" Noah tilted his head, listening intently.

"At the east gate, awaiting my orders, O king."

"Bring them here!"

The captain and his guard turned to obey.

Amulon shouted, "Wait!"

He hurried to the king and whispered again. Noah smirked, then nodded.

"Change that last order," Noah said. "When the sun is at its highest point, I want you to release them. Let them go."

"Release them?"

"Yes, and let anyone else go that desires. Do not detain anyone." He paused, his small eyes looked out at the captain from above the folds of skin.

"Is that clear?" he shouted.

Gideon nodded and hurried from the room.

Amulon smiled. "We will have Alma and all his people," he snorted. Turning to Ukiahah, a lesser priest, he asked. "Name me a family loyal to the throne."

Ukiahah shrugged, "Tao and his wife are loyal."

"Are they smart enough to follow directions?"

"I believe so."

"I don't want your belief," Noah growled. "Are they smart enough?"

"Yes," Ukiahah answered, appearing intimidated.

"Then get them," Amulon commanded. "Have them report to us immediately."

Ukiahah hurried from the room.

* * *

Each day Alma taught, reading to the people from the scriptures, challenging them to full fellowship. He reminded them that such full fellowship would only come through processes of repentance and faith in the Lord.

More families joined the small congregation at the Waters of Mormon. Alma was kept busy teaching them about baptism and then baptizing them. Each night as he came home to his family he would fall into bed, exhausted.

Abimolam came one night and put his arms around Alma's neck.

"My son, I don't want to act like a mother hen, and I know that often-times young people don't like advice of those of us who are older, but I would like to help you."

"What is it, father?" Alma answered. "You know that now I do accept and follow your advice."

Abimolam smiled. "I would like to tell you a story. Do you recall from the scriptures the experience of Moses leading the children of Israel from Egypt to the Promised Land?"

Alma nodded affirmatively.

"You might remember the burdens of office became so heavy that Moses was always tired and never had time for his wife and children."

Alma nodded again, still not sure of his father's point.

"The story goes that Jethro, Moses' father-in-law, came to visit him and his family. Moses went out to meet Jethro, bowed and kissed him."

Alma kept looking blankly at him.

Abimolam was obviously enjoying himself. "Jethro followed Moses around, observing what he was doing. He watched as Moses sat in judgment of his people and gave counsel from morning to evening. Jethro was amazed. He finally asked Moses what he was doing. Moses told him that he was teaching the people the laws of God and making decisions of judgment between them when disputes arose."

"What does that have to do with me?" asked Alma.

"I am getting to that. Jethro told Moses that what he was doing wasn't good, that he would 'surely wear away.' Then he said, 'I will give you counsel. Select some good and able men to whom you can delegate some of your responsibilities. Let them judge the people. Have them bring big matters to you and smaller matters to those you appoint. That will make it easier for you and better for your people.' "

He smiled. "Moses listened to his father-in-law, choosing able men and making them heads over the people, delegating to them some of his responsibilities."

Alma nodded in understanding.

"My son, you are a Moses to this people. My advice would be that of Jethro. Find some able men who can share with you burdens of leadership. Delegate to them certain responsibilities. This will give you greater opportunity to serve."

By candlelight, Alma took out his copy of the writings of the brass plates. He found and read the words of Moses and Jethro of which his father had spoken. "Rulers of thousands, rulers of hundreds, rulers of fifties, and rulers of tens," he mused. "Moses led thousands of people. Surely I can lead my few hundreds. I shall choose priests for each fifty people."

He looked at his sleeping wife, then knelt by her side. "Father, thank you for letting my father be Thy spokesman. If it be Thy will, help me name priests to whom I can delegate responsibilities for this people."

Sleep did not come for some time. As he lay there, names of nine men came to his mind. Contented, he fell into a deep sleep.

At first light, Alma circuited the encampment. Morning dew soon had his sandals and legs soaking wet. There was freshness in the air. The forest smelled clean and earthy.

Alma zigzagged his way up the valley. Families that had come without tents had erected crude shelters of branches and mud. Tents and shelters were scattered through the forest. Campfires burned brightly, lighted from the previous night's coals. An aroma of woodsmoke and meals cooking filled the air. Family members, draped in blankets of assorted colors, huddled around fires. Alma stopped at each fire. He greeted people warmly and told them to meet at noon at the meeting place.

Hours passed as he visited with his people. He was amazed to see how the group had grown, almost double what it had been at the time of the first baptism. People arrived daily from the city of Nephi. He now affectionately called the people the "Church of Christ."

After a leisurely breakfast with Esther, Zoram and Abimolam, he sat and read scriptures. The puppy lay at his feet, licking his bare ankles. As noon hour approached, he saw people drifting to the meeting ground. He put away his papers, and with Esther at his side, walked to the meeting.

When all were assembled he called upon his father to pray. Abimolam blessed the people and called down powers of Heaven to sustain them. He prayed for a special blessing on Alma and the things which he would do this day. Alma smiled. His father knew what he planned and so did the Lord. Alma was glad he had the blessings of both of his fathers.

He stood before the people, looked at them intently before he spoke. Then he began. "I desire that Amalakiahah, Balzar, Nephihah, Helam, my father, Zephany, Tapiah, Amarta and Zebulon come forward."

Each threaded his way to the front. Alma clasped hands with them, then turned to the people. "The voice of the Lord, through me, has called these men to be priests to administer and serve you. They are just men and will consecrate their time to your service."

A hum of whispering surged through the congregation.

Alma held up his hand for silence. "Is there anyone here who would not support these men in this sacred and holy calling?"

He looked at the congregation. Not one hand was raised. He turned to the men, all of whom seemed surprised except for Abimolam.

"I will meet with you afterwards to talk about responsibilities. You may take your places now with your families."

He preached for an hour, commanding the people to observe the Sabbath day, which was a new concept for most of the people. He explained that the Sabbath would be one day set aside in every week for people to gather together to worship their God.

He commanded people to impart of their substance to any who had need. A feeling of love and unity seemed to emanate from the congregation. Alma knew they loved him and loved the word of God which he preached to them.

After the meeting, most returned to their tents. The nine men Alma had selected remained behind with their families. Alma called Abimolam forward and laid an arm across his father's shoulder. "My father was ordained in the days of Zeniff," he said. "I would like him to help me ordain each of you to the priesthood."

After ordaining the other eight men to their calling as priests in the young church, Alma spoke to them. "Since I began my preaching, you have all listened faithfully. Now you will be preaching what I have taught you. Do not deviate from those things. Keep the Gospel simple and pure. Teach doctrines of repentance and faith in God. Search the scriptures and do not teach anything that cannot be found therein."

Hesitantly Tapiah stepped forward. "Alma, perhaps I am not suited for this holy calling. I have not learned to read."

Alma smiled. "Thank you, Tapiah. There are probably several of you that have not been trained to read. Father?" Abimolam stepped up. "Will you teach those who need to learn to read, just as you taught me so many years ago?"

Abimolam nodded and sat down.

Alma taught them duties. "Your most important responsibility is to teach the Gospel. Keep the love of God in your heart at all times. There shall be no contention between you, or between you and any member. If contentions do arise come to me quickly so they can be worked out.

"Each will be responsible for fifty people. We will make assignments later with your suggestions. Care for your families, look over them, help them solve problems. Help people knit their hearts together in love and unity.

"Do not ask anyone for support. Continue the things you are doing to support your families. The Lord will bless you materially as well as spiritually. You will have abundance if you keep the commandments of God. In addition, through your faithfulness you will wax strong in spirit, gain greater knowledge of God, and teach with power and authority."

Chapter 4

Exodus

"Bring Tao and his wife!" Noah's shout echoed through palace corridors.

The king's guards hastened in with an elderly-looking couple. The wife was gray-haired and wrinkled, her lips set in a perpetual tight-lipped frown. Tao's fringe of white hair ringed his wrinkled and freckled head. His thinning hair made his ears seem abnormally large. Nervously shuffling their sandals on the marble floor, the couple stood before Noah's throne.

"Speak up, man," commanded Amulon. "What did you see?"

His voice wavering, Tao recounted his experience.

He and his wife had feigned belief in Alma's preaching. They left at noon with the other converts, traveled till dark, camped at night near a wild forest. The next night they arrived at the Waters of Mormon where they found many people.

"Alma was there preaching." Tao said.

Amulon turned to the exultant Noah. "There, my king. We have the traitors where they can be destroyed."

Noah dismissed Tao and his wife, then called Bilbah, the army commander. "Tomorrow," he said. "take your army to the Waters of Mormon and destroy everyone there except Alma and Helam. I want no others left alive. Bring Alma and Helam to me."

General Bilbah saluted and left.

"And what of Alma and Helam?" asked Amulon.

Noah sneered. "They will learn consequences of stirring up a rebellion against me. They shall taste a death similar to that of their friend, Abinadi."

Smiling wickedly, Amulon returned to his chair.

* * *

Alma.

Alma awoke from a deep sleep. He looked around. The tent was empty except for Esther and Zoram and they both slept soundly. He supposed he must have imagined the voice. The dog was sitting next to Zoram's pallet, his ears cocked forward. Alma put his head back on the pillow. The voice came again, *Alma.*

Then he knew the voice. He bowed his head. "What is it, Lord?"

Alma, King Noah is sending his army to destroy you. Move from this place. I will guide you.

"Yes, Lord."

He awakened Esther and Zoram. Quickly explaining to them what happened, he asked Esther to strike the tent, pack their things, and be ready to go. He held Zoram's little head between his hands.

"My son, help your mother. Will you do that?"

Little Zoram replied, "I'll help, father." The puppy, sensing excitement, hopped around Zoram's feet on its stubby legs.

Alma laced up his sandals and left the tent. He was glad he had previously located the leaders' tents. He hurried through the night, calling forth one after another, explaining the situation and instructing them to get packed and ready to leave the valley.

"Notify your assigned families!" and he was off again in dark night.

* * *

Esther was sick. She sat on the tormented roots of a mahogany tree listening to voices of frogs and insects as they raised a cacophony of sound around her. Above, in the tree tops, birds and monkeys commented rudely on the intrusion.

Since leaving the Waters of Mormon, she had struggled for days through deep forest. The foliage had changed from scrub and pine forest to a scented tangle of mahogany, sapodilla and bracken. Temperature and humidity increased. To her dismay, with the increase of temperature came swarms of mosquitoes, scattering like pollen from the inhibiting undergrowth. The sun vanished as their progress was roofed over by sweating branches and vines. They crossed slimy swamps where the stench of rotting logs nauseated her. Even sweet smells of numerous wild flowers which she had always loved now made her stomach feel queasy.

She was thankful they were making their journey during dry season. She shuddered as she imagined how miserable they would be fighting their way through the forest during the wet season with dreary rain dripping through the trees.

As she rested, she watched the alert, angular progress of a lizard through leaves on the damp jungle floor. The lizard seemed to sense her presence and darted into a cave of leaves, its tail, yellow-gray, still obvious.

The call came to resume their journey. Esther wearily stood and began walking. She could see only ten paces in front of her and only half that to either side. She felt closed in, desiring to scream. With no sunlight penetrating the thickness of the jungle she could not judge the time of day. Briars and creepers and vines grew thickly between tree trunks. Walking exhausted her even after men hacked a path.

Vines reached from above to caress her face and neck. She imagined herself totally vulnerable. The file before her passed through a thick, swirling nebulae of mosquitos, so teeming they obscured the jungle walls in opaque mist.

The night had even been miserable for her. Though snuggling with Alma and surrounded by his followers, she shivered as she listened to strident wild animal cries. Fear, a hard knot in her stomach, stayed with her all day. Several times she cried out as she saw beady eyes of huge yellow and black-striped snakes watching her from overhanging branches. Esther was not sure she could take much more. And now her stomach was churning within her. Tears of self-pity ran down her cheeks. She angrily pushed some branches aside, scratching her bare arms. A chattering erupted above her and she glanced up to see dozens of red monkeys swinging along in easy rhythm above the refugees.

She admitted the forest was beautiful. If I weren't hurting so badly, she thought, I could really enjoy its beauty. She marveled at giant leaves which were as broad across as Alma was tall, and contrasting petite leaves of tiny trailside plants with clear, red fruits and almost invisible white flowers. She often looked up at the shadowy world above her. Brambles, gnarled trunks and dark vine curtains concealed much from her view. Cedars, mahoganies, sapodillas and breadnuts towered above the tangle, their great branches punctuated by dark bromeliad starbursts. So many colored birds and animals was awesome.

If only Alma would spend more time with her and little Zoram, she thought. Thinking of Zoram brought her up short. Where was he? He and the dog had been right behind her. She turned quickly and Helam almost bumped into her. He smiled reassuringly at her and inclined his head. There was Zoram, riding stoically on Helam's pack. He waved and smiled at her, his eyes merry above his rosy cheeks. Annah, following behind Helam, smiled at her.

"Isn't he too heavy?" she asked.

"Not a bit," Helam replied. "Zoram is like a son to me. Do not worry, I will take care of him."

Esther turned and continued her trudging. Stomach pains renewed their harshness and she compressed her lips to avoid moaning aloud. Alma had worries enough, attempting to protect his more than four hundred people, without worrying about her.

The next time the column stopped for a rest, she turned to Helam, "Why is it we are made to suffer like this? It seems to me if the Lord wants us to follow His word He would just protect us from King Noah's army . . . ."

She waved her arm in frustration as she continued, " . . . Instead of having us almost die in this cursed wilderness!"

Helam appeared to reflect for a moment before answering. "In the past, Esther, whenever God wanted to purify His people, He sent them on a journey." He looked at Esther with compassion.

"For example, you will remember Abraham's and Jacob's journeys to the Promised Land; the journey of Moses and children of Israel from Egypt; and in our own history, the journey of Lehi and his family to this promised land; the journey of Mosiah and his people to Zarahemla; and the journey of Zeniff and our forefathers back to the Land of Nephi. Now we are on our own journey. I feel each journey tests the depth of people's conviction. Migration is a purging, purifying process which polishes and grinds people exceedingly fine."

Esther lost the analogy. She was thankful when Helam took both her hands and explained. "As I understand it, if God wants to raise up a people dedicated to serving him, He tests them in the wilderness. There they learn to work together or die. Wilderness experience teaches people to walk by faith or fail. Trials are ordained by God to strengthen His chosen people."

As she pondered that, her attention was drawn to a cluster of insects bouncing up and down in a sunlight shaft filtering through tree cover overhead. She observed as they rose a few inches, dropped back to tops of bushes, rose again in what seemed to be aritualistic dance. They bumped each other going up and coming down as if they could not see where they were going. Most stayed together in a small vertical column, but as time went on, ranks thinned until only a few remained to continue their ceaseless up and down motion. The rest had disappeared into shade.

Perhaps this is what Helam is talking about, she mused. Sometimes what we do seems as purposeless as insects going up and down, but if we deviate from light, we are lost.

* * *

At column front, Alma cut and chopped his way through dense forest. His arms were weary from the constant cutting and slashing, but he kept hacking. He had great faith in the Lord's direction, but the responsibility for those following was heavy upon him. What if they didn't find a good place to settle? What if many died? What if King Noah's soldiers found them? Or Lamanites? As doubts assailed him, he forcibly put them away from him. He must walk by faith. There could be no doubt or fear. No What ifs! he said to himself. The Lord would provide. He kept a constant prayer in his mind. Oh, God, lead this people to safety. Guide us to the place where we can live our religion free from fear.

Their progress had been so slow. Obstinate sheep and goats darting off into heavy timber required much time to get back on the trail. Alma was grateful the plodding burros had given them no problems. Without burros, they would not have been able to bring their heavy tents. Packs on the backs of his people would have been too heavy for them to bear.

He cut through the last underbrush and broke out of the forest. Grassland extended for leagues, broken only by scattered, symmetrical, fan-shaped ceiba trees with their tall and slender, bottle-shaped trunks.

He crossed a patch of calf-high wild anise, crushing out fragrance with each step of his sandals. Like a huge cloth billowing in the wind, a flock of swallows swooped down, turning on themselves. The sun shone obliquely from the west, its rays probing at the wooded ridge above him and the blue-purple flanks of the distant volcanoes to the right.

People gathered about Alma. Flocks scattered and grazed peacefully on lush grass. He looked around. The clearing led down to a beautiful basin protected on two sides by tall mountains. The basin was a hidden retreat. He was suddenly aware of Esther's presence. He put his arm around her. She snuggled against him gratefully.

* * *

Esther was comforted by Alma's arm. She breathed in beauties of the scene before her. After the horrible forest, anything seemed beautiful. The valley floor was covered with flowers of every hue: purples and yellows and whites. Huge gorgeous butterflies, looking like flying flowers, swooped and flitted before them.

She shuddered quietly, then bit her lip, trying to ignore pains gnawing at her stomach. She shook her head, then looked at Alma, a question in her eyes.

Shrugging his shoulders, he answered her unspoken question. "I don't know, my dear. Our people are tired and this would be a good resting place. But I am not sure we are far enough away from Noah and his armies." He thought for a moment. "We have been gone eight days from the Waters of Mormon. Perhaps we can stay in this place."

She attempted to stifle the low moan, but it escaped her lips as a pain hit her. She writhed in pain.

"What's the matter?" Alma almost shouted his concern.

"It is nothing," she whispered hoarsely.

"Nothing?"

"Perhaps it was something I ate." She smiled up at him.

He turned to the group. "Will someone bring my father. Esther is ill."

Abimolam, a concerned look on his face, hurried to them.

Again she said, "It's nothing. Just something I ate." As she spoke, another spasm hit her. She doubled over, grimacing in pain.

Alma threw a blanket on the ground, then gently lowered her to it. Abimolam knelt beside her, poking and prodding, observing where she was tender.

Her husband stood above her. He asked, "Are you all right?"

She nodded mutely, tears dimming her eyes.

Alma looked down the valley. He motioned Helam to him. "Father and I will stop here for awhile with Esther. My friend, take the people. I see sunlight glinting on water. Set up camp there."

Esther watched as Alma patted little Zoram's head, scratched the dog behind the ears, then turned his attention back to her.

Abimolam reached into his pouch and extracted several shreds of bark. He crumbled them between his palms then mixed them with his gourd of water. "Drink this, my child," he said, holding up her head.

After drinking the herb, Esther felt drowsy. She strained to catch what Alma and his father were saying, then she heard no more.

* * *

Abimolam stood as soon as he saw that Esther was asleep. Alma stood with him, an inquiring look on his face.

"I think it is her appendix," Abimolam said. "The cinchona bark I gave her has put her to sleep."

"What can we do?"

"Physicians in Lehi have learned surgery to remove such diseased organs," he said calmly.

"But we are not in the City of Lehi," Alma said with exasperation.

"I know. The only other thing I can think of is sap of the balsam tree. It has healing and antiseptic powers."

"Do you have some?"

"No."

"How do I recognize such a tree? I will find it."

"Balsam trees are easy to recognize: they have graceful branches spreading high and wide, but the search might take days. Balsam is not a common tree. They do not grow in groves, but are loners." He looked at his son, a half-smile on his wrinkled but cherubic face.

"Father, we do not have time to search. Esther needs help now."

"Then I suggest you use your priesthood."

"What?"

"Use your priesthood. Give her a blessing."

"But how?"

"Bless her through your priesthood and in the name of Jesus Christ who is to come."

Alma finally realized what his father had been working towards. "Will you assist me?" he asked.

"Yes, my son." Abimolam seemed satisfied.

Alma and his father again knelt beside sleeping Esther. They bent over and laid their hands on her head. Alma noted how hot her brow was.

He prayed. "Father in Heaven, thou hast been with us in all our endeavors." Words of praise and thanksgiving fell from his lips. Then he added his heartfelt blessing: "Now, Father, Thy beloved daughter and my loyal and chaste wife is ill. As you are aware, it was she who first believed Abinadi and led me to him. She has total faith in Thee and deserves to be healed. With complete faith in Thy powers to heal, we therefore ask Thy healing power be upon her. Bless her that her body may throw off the illness afflicting her. Bless her that her fever may leave. Bless her that she may have health and strength to continue on with our journey. Bless her that she may live to bear more children for our family."

He paused. Tears from his closed eyes fell on his sleeping wife's face. "Bless her, Father, that she may continue here on earth as my devoted and beloved wife."

Esther moaned softly.

Authority rang in Alma's voice. "Father, through the power of Thy priesthood, we command this illness to leave her body that she may be left whole and well. And through that priesthood, we seal this blessing in the name of Him who has been prophesied to come, even Thy Son, Jesus Christ, Amen."

Alma and his father continued to kneel by Esther's prostrate body. Alma's head drooped. He looked up, right into his father's moist eyes. Abimolam raised his hands from Esther's head and placed them on Alma's shoulders.

"My son, I felt the Lord's answer as you prayed. Esther will be well."

* * *

Alma, Abimolam and Esther arrived at the lake much later than the others. The sun was setting behind the mountains. Esther had awakened and insisted on walking with them to the encampment. She seemed free from pain and the fever had left her.

Alma observed that the lake water was pure and fresh. Meadows surrounding the lake provided excellent grazing for livestock. Pine forests rimmed hillsides, dotted here and there with taller mahogany trees. Thick vegetation sealed the forest's edge. Alma bent down and sifted some black, volcanic soil through his fingers: a perfect soil for their crops.

Helam had done his job well. Several men and boys were already fishing in the lake which could provide fresh fish for supper. Others were digging pits for latrines while each family erected its shelter. By the time Alma arrived, his tent was erected.

To help avoid detection, Helam had located the tent camp in a wooded cove up a small ravine from the lake. A stream ran down the ravine's center, a beautiful setting.

Brilliantly colored birds flew overhead. Jewel-toned hummingbirds zipped through the meadow, stopping sporadically at open throats of low-lying flowers. Pinkish-colored herons stood one-legged in lake shallows. Alma absorbed all the sights and sounds of this valley with its mountains and forests.

A voice whispered to his consciousness. *Here you and your people will live for many seasons. This shall be your land.*

Alma called the sweaty and dirty Helam to him. A broad smile lighted his face. Alma clapped him on the shoulder, "My friend, God has told me this shall be our home. We have traveled for eight days from the Waters of Mormon. If we are a righteous people, King Noah will not be able to find us here." Again he looked over the lake and its peaceful setting. He motioned with his arm. "Here we will prosper as we rear our families in peace."

Helam's eyes had a faraway look. "Yes, here we will raise up a righteous generation for the Lord."

* * *

A few weeks later, Esther lay quietly on the mat beside Alma. From his breathing she knew he was still awake.

She whispered. "Alma."

"What, dear."

"Remember the day we arrived in this valley?"

"Um huh."

"Remember how sick I was?"

Alma turned to her, and stroked her hair. "How could I forget. You really had me worried."

"Abimolam thought my appendix was inflamed?"

"Yes."

She smiled as she detected curiosity in his voice. "It wasn't my appendix, my dear. Instead, we are going to have another child."

A sharp, breathy intake was the only sound she heard, then Alma enfolded her in his big arms.

* * *

Days and weeks became months. The secluded valley had been good for the people and they soon relaxed, no longer fearing Noah's pursuit. Each Sabbath Alma read scriptures or taught them words which the Lord put in his mind. For the refugees it was a time of peace and thanksgiving.

To free Alma's time for handling religious and spiritual matters, Helam had volunteered to assume many responsibilities for the encampment. Under his direction, people began to build permanent log and stone houses and to till the earth.

People were industrious. Men, older boys, and stronger women working in teams, cut and dragged trees from the nearby forest for their homes. Work was back-breaking but men were encouraged by knowing that soon their homes would be built. Craftsmen searched out dark red mahogany trees and built furniture. Several men were gone many days exploring and looking for wood. They came back really excited after finding "springtime" trees covered with profuse yellow blossoms. Light cream-colored wood of the springtime tree made a delightful contrast when laminated with darker mahogany.

While some of the men built homes and furniture, Esther and other women went with younger children into the forest to gather berries and edible roots. They also gathered fruit from ceiba trees in the valley. They stripped fiber from the fruit, dried the fiber, and used it for their mattresses. Some searched out trees where bees made their hives, harvesting sticky sweet honey for community use.

Women and children cared for gardens. Cotton, tomatoes, sweet potatoes, squash, black beans and pumpkins all grew in the dark and fertile soil.

Abimolam, schooled in herbs, sent expeditions out to get bark from conacosta trees and to find the scarce balsam. He instructed men on how to cut bark to get sap running. Abimolam boiled sap until crude extract settled to the bottom. He poured off water and heated the residue to purify it. This extract he saved for healing. Men found maguey and henequen cactus and agave. Women mashed plant fibers to make ropes and sandals.

Helam took men high into the forest on a hunting expedition. They found deer and peccaries in abundance. Close to camp, fat monkeys were easy to catch. Turtles abounded in the lake, providing meat and delicious eggs to eat. In addition, their bony shells were used to make combs, jewelry and other beautiful objects.

First harvest was a time of celebration. With storage bins full, men fashioned flutes and whistles from willows, drums from hollow logs, and rattles from gourds. Dancing and feasting went long into the night. Alma and Esther danced for the first time since Abinadi's street meeting. Esther clung to Alma like mist to morning grass, weaving to pulsating music.

After the harvest, during rainy season, Esther and other women spun cotton into thread. They dyed thread with dyes they obtained from indigo plants and small cochineal insects. From the threads they wove coarse cloth into coats and capes for men, and dresses and shawls for women.

Alma used the lull to find wild fig trees. He stripped as much bark as he could carry, then spent several weeks cleaning, soaking, and separating it until he had thin sheets of paper. He didn't quit until he felt he had enough writing materials for several years.

After homes were completed, Alma and Helam began a project to build a meeting house. They patterned the church after Nephi's temple.

Abimolam was not strong enough to help with building or hunting, and Alma was concerned about him. He had seen too many older people lose interest in life and wither away. Abimolam had helped with herbs, but now he needed something else to do to keep busy. Then the answer came to Alma. Family tradition was that each child be taught as a scribe. Zoram was only five, but he was old enough to begin learning the languages of his fathers. Soon boy and grandfather were sitting together in the shade of a pine tree, scribing on a piece of clay.

Alma felt great pride in his firstborn son. Zoram's body was strong and well-sculptured. He seemed broad to Alma, and even his small, bowed legs added to an impression of great strength. His red hair seemed to fly in every direction. Alma smiled. The dog—Zoram named it Bones—was almost full grown and never left Zoram's side. The two made a good pair. They loved to explore lake shore and forest.

As Alma watched, he knew Zoram would rather be running through the forest with Bones than studying Hebrew and Egyptian. Zoram had expressed no interest in being a scribe. He probably would not like the instruction, but Alma felt the schooling would be good for both Zoram and Abimolam.

Within weeks Abimolam was teaching a regular group of children. Alma smiled with delight. Their village had its first school of scribes and his father now saw new purpose for his life.

Esther delivered their second child. The baby was a dark-haired girl. Alma tenderly held the baby and named her Netta.

On his next trip to his sacred forest glade Alma knelt and prayed. "Praise Thee for this new little one in our family. Praise Thee for peace."

Chapter 5

Land of Helam

Voices buzzed and the whispering in the congregation disturbed Alma. Usually when he taught, the people were more attentive. He looked over his congregation, then beyond them, seeing homes and the lake in the background. Even after delegating much authority to his priests, he felt the total weight of responsibility for this people.

Balzar stood, indicating his desire to speak. Alma nodded.

"Alma, through your leadership we have escaped from King Noah and have settled in this beautiful valley. You have labored beside us from the beginning. We feel it is fitting that you become our king."

A chorus of "ayes."

Alma motioned for quiet.

"My beloved people," he said. "Thank you for wanting me to be your king. If circumstances were different, I would be glad to serve as king, but for now, it is not suitable for us to have a king. The Lord has said, 'Ye shall not esteem one flesh above another.' "

Helam stood, waiting for the babble to cease. He spoke in a serious tone. "Alma, the people love you. They want you as king."

"Thank you." Alma said. "If it were possible to always have a just man to be king, then setting up a kingship would be appropriate. But have you forgotten so soon the wickedness of King Noah and his priests? Even I was caught in his web of sin."

"But you are a righteous man," shouted someone.

"Yes," smiled Alma, "so was Zeniff. But his righteousness didn't extend to his son, Noah. By God's power we have been delivered from Noah's evil influence. I for one would not want to place our people in a position that such a thing could happen again.

"We cannot jeopardize our freedom." He paused in deep thought. Looking up, he continued. "We have lived as free men since leaving the Land of Nephi because of our willingness to stand up for our beliefs.

"Freedom is such a precious thing. To bless our children with freedom, we will need to be constantly on guard. Stand fast in the liberty which we now possess. I exhort you to trust no man to be a king over you."

Alma recalled a scripture. "Our forefather, Jacob, speaking of the gentiles who would later settle this land, said: 'This land shall be a land of liberty unto the Gentiles, and there shall be no kings upon the land.' If kings are not appropriate for the Gentiles, are they appropriate for us?"

Helam stood again. "Alma, we need a leader. What shall we call him, if not king?"

"I agree our people need a leader," Alma said. "A leader who is a man of God—who walks in His ways and keeps His commandments. God has called me to be your high priest. That is sufficient for me. Choose from among you one who can be a leader. Then let him be elected by the voice of the people."

Amalakiahah, one of Alma's first converts, stood. "Helam has shown great leadership in directing our camp in this place. I say we choose Helam."

There was a chorus of "Ayes."

Alma looked over the assemblage. "Are all of you willing to have Helam be your leader, subject to the voice of the people?"

"Aye," came the echoing response.

"So be it," Alma said, motioning for Helam. "I concur and I believe God does also." He looked intently at them. "Always remember, no teacher or leader should be appointed by this people without the Lord's approval." He turned to Helam. "Do you accept this responsibility?"

"If the people and the Lord want me to continue to serve them," Helam said, "I am willing to do so."

Alma looked over his people. "You have chosen wisely. With Helam's leadership and with continued obedience to God's commandments, we will prosper in this land. So has the Lord promised. But I exhort you to continue in your faith. Let no spirit of contention disturb the relationship you have with any of the people in this village. Contention is of the devil. The Lord's way is to love each other as you do yourselves."

Zephany stood, his brows wrinkled, obviously concerned about something. He spoke up immediately. "Alma, we have not chosen a name for our city. The traditions of our people have been to name a land and city after the leader." He paused and looked with obvious embarrassment at Helam. "I was going to propose we name this the Land of Alma. Now I am confused."

Alma smiled. "Thank you. I have been honored enough already. Name the land after our new leader: the Land of Helam, and the City of Helam."

He looked around, accepting the nodding of heads as affirmation of his proposal. He walked to Helam.

"My friend," he said. "This land will always be called after your name."

"I will live up to your trust in me, and to the honor you have bestowed upon me," Helam answered humbly.

* * *

Westward, the high white cone which the people had named Tanza, "the smoking one," dominated the horizon. Alma watched as the setting sun illuminated it, first in gold and finally in soft violet. As he walked towards the lake, a warm south wind tumbling through the forest and sounds of the village formed a muted background for his footsteps. He sighed.

Having priesthood leaders gave him more time with his family, but it seemed more and more time was needed to teach, supervise, and listen to problems. He realized the importance of spending time with his son, and he tried to be with him often. They had taken time to gather wild berries, dig edible roots, or sit under trees and talk. Sometimes they walked around the lake. Bones was good at sniffing out turtle nests. Finding turtle eggs was always a thrill for young Zoram. But it seemed to Alma there never was enough time.

To complete Zoram's education, Alma engaged Amalakiahah, an artisan in the City of Nephi, to teach him a craft. Alma traded animal skins with Amalakiahah in exchange for teaching. He watched them through their first project. Amalakiahah took Zoram hunting turtles. They killed a large one, removed the heavy shell, filled it full of water, then heated it over the fire. When the water had boiled for some time, they removed the shell from the fire and pressed it flat under heavy weights. When it was cooled and dry, Amalakiahah and Zoram polished the flat shell with sand until it was a translucent golden yellow color dotted with rich brown spots. Amalakiahah taught Zoram to cut the shell into pieces of desired size, then to shape and cut it into the objects they wanted. Zoram's first project was a comb for his mother.

When he presented it to her, she hugged him to her and cried.

"I will always wear it with pride," she said.

* * *

Alma diligently recorded the people's history as rainy season followed dry season, marking the passing of years. He noted children born in the community. He wrote down revelations he received from the Lord and sermons he gave.

Another daughter, Leesa, was born to their family. What joy she added, especially since Alma knew that Esther was approaching the end of her child-bearing years.

"I will be satisfied with my son and two daughters," he said. But secretly he yearned for another son. Zoram, his eldest, had indicated a reluctance to be a priest, preferring instead to work with his hands or to be a warrior. Alma wondered if the Lord would bless him with a son who would

follow in his footsteps; one who would be willing to accept spiritual leadership of the people.

The community prospered. Through the years they lived in righteousness and total faith. There was a closeness and unity among them.

In those years, only one item of sadness came. Alma's father, Abimolam,
died. He was in his seventieth year, and Alma was pleased he had been
able to live as long as he had. Through his father he had gained great
strength and spiritual insight.

They buried Abimolam on a hillside overlooking the lake. His father's
grave was a hallowed spot for Alma and he went there often to meditate
and pray—drawing strength from his father's close spirit.

* * *

Esther was not sure she shared Alma's enthusiasm about the community.
As the city of Helam grew, Alma's responsibilities increased. Houses filled
the little valley and extended around part of the lake. Dozens of fishing
boats made of woven reeds lined the beach. Vegetable gardens beside the
village and terraced into hillsides gave physical guidance to the people
while Alma was kept busy giving spiritual guidance.

Esther lay on her woven mat. Sleep would not come. Why was she feeling so concerned? She knew Alma loved her. She had a fine home. She
was respected by the other women in the community. She had three
healthy and beautiful children. What more could she want? The answer
was not difficult for her to perceive. She wanted more of Alma's time.
As chief priest it seemed he was gone all of the time. "So-and-so needs
my help," or "that one broke her leg," or . . . Oh, the list was endless.

Why couldn't she just be happy with what she had? Alma was doing
the Lord's will and that was that! Or was it? Why did she have such nagging doubts?

Her restless turning awakened Alma. He rolled over and put his arm
around her, snuggling her close. She was grateful for his love. She knew
she shouldn't trouble Alma with her concerns, but . . . .

"Alma."

"What is it, my love."

Silence.

"Is something the matter?"

Tears welled in Esther's eyes and ran down her cheeks onto the bed.

"You're crying."

"It is nothing."

"Something is bothering you. Please tell me."

Silence.

"Please?"

A pent-up flood of words erupted from Esther's lips. "Everyone else seems more important to you than the children and I. All day I never get to see you, and as soon as you get home all you want to do is eat and go to bed."

Esther buried her face in Alma's chest. She could feel his heart beating strongly as she waited for his answer.

When he spoke, his voice was quiet and introspective. "I can see I have been neglecting you."

"Oh, Alma. It isn't that. I know how busy you are being high priest over all the people and hunting and fishing and raising enough food to feed us. I guess I'm selfish but I need some of your time, too. All I do is weave and hoe and cook and sew. And Zoram . . . ."

"What of Zoram?"

"He is sixteen. He needs your time."

Esther hoped she hadn't hurt Alma's feelings. He took a long time to answer.

"I have neglected the most important part of my life. That will change."

Esther snuggled close to him, drawing comfort from his large, strong body.

During the next few days she noticed a change. Alma was more considerate of her, taking her for walks by the lake, practicing swordplay with Zoram, helping Netta with her chores and carrying seven-year-old Leesa around on his shoulders.

One day he hurried into the house. "I have a great idea."

Esther was too surprised to answer.

"Let's pack a lunch and climb Tanza. Few of our people have been to the top of the volcano and it would be a great adventure."

Fear constricted her throat. "Wouldn't that be dangerous?"

"The volcano smokes but does not erupt; like a dog that barks but does not bite."

Zoram was all for the idea. Hiking up a volcano sounded like great adventure to him.

Next morning they started. Alma carried little Leesa on his shoulders. Esther looked at the volcano's immense bulk etched against the bright blue sky. Could they really climb clear to its top? What if it erupted while they were on it? From her first step she continued to worry.

They hiked through dense pine forests, sticking to trails Alma knew from his hunting trips. The trail was gravelly under their sandals. Then they climbed through crumbled volcanic cinders and tumbled boulders of porous lava rock and pumice. The forest thinned as they climbed higher, finally giving way to patches of manzanita and scrub brush.

Zoram and Bones ranged back and forth across the trail. Sadly, Esther noticed how slow and awkward Bones was becoming. He had grown old

but the dog was still Zoram's closest companion. She watched as Zoram
stopped and let Bones rest, then with both hands scratched both sides
of the dog's back.

When Alma stopped for lunch, Esther was ready. Her feet were sore
and her legs tired. She gasped for breath. Zoram and Netta looked as fresh
as ever, and though he was carrying Leesa, Alma was not even breathing
hard.

"How much farther to the top?" she wheezed.

"We must be at least half way," Alma replied.

She moaned, then looked back the way they had come. Below her lay
a breathtaking panorama. The tumultous green of the forest blended with
the lighter green of valley and the deep blue of the lake. Overhead the
sky was bright azure with dazzling sun. The whole scene gave Esther a
feeling of awe. Two ruby-red dragonflies chased themselves across the
rocks and settled on the swaying stem of a nearby plant. Esther had never
observed such beauty. Now she wished she didn't have to leave this spot.
But after eating their meat and fruit lunch, Alma seemed anxious to be
off. Zoram, Bones and Netta were already a hundred paces up the hillside.
Reluctantly she stood and began climbing.

With the exception of rest stops, she climbed without speaking; mainly
because she had no breath with which to speak, partly because she felt
a closeness with her husband which required no words. Leesa made up
for her mother's silence by chattering incessantly. Zoram, Bones, and Netta
were always out in front, or exploring side trails; out of speaking range.

As the family climbed higher, exquisite little alpine plants blossomed
in rock crevices—tiny stars and trumpets of red and blue and yellow and
purple. Alma pointed out a coyote and her pups loping around the hillside,
and there were always hummingbirds and macaws flying overhead.

As they approached the summit, rays of the dying sun turned everything
to gold. Alma climbed the last few feet to the rim, then pulled Esther up
just as the last color faded from the sky. They were greeted on top by wind
which rushed at them, tugging at their hair and clothes.

Esther felt a flash of fear, then calmed herself as she felt the stalwart
man at her side. Zoram, Netta, and Leesa, too, had quieted and were standing by them. Bones pressed tightly against Zoram's leg. A strong smell,
as if of rotten eggs, hung in the air.

"We will find a flat place where we can unroll our mats," Alma said.
"Then, as tired as you are, you will sleep well."

Esther wasn't sure she could sleep, but Alma was right, she was tired.
She listened to night sounds around her: mice scurrying to and fro, the
whistle of bird's wings as they darted through the darkness, the soft
rhythmic chuffing noise of the volcano. She slept.

Morning arrived in a glorious way. Never had Esther seen such a beautiful and inspiring sunrise. The sun leaped from behind the horizon, lighting up high white clouds with the brilliance of fire, all tones of orange, yellow, pink and violet. With the sun in the sky, the broad expanse of the land far below opened up to her: forests and valleys and lakes and rivers. She pointed wordlessly. Alma saw it, too. The glinting of the sun on a broad expanse of water to the west: the west sea of which they had heard but never before seen.

After several moments of gazing and wondering, Esther responded to the insistent tugs of Zoram on her arm. They walked across the wide rim towards where smoke and steam seemed to be rising out of the ground. As they neared, the rotten-egg smell became stronger, apparently part of the steam they were seeing.

The crater's edge yawned before them. Esther gazed fearfully into the hole, then gasped as she looked at the precipitous sides which ended with a perfectly formed dark gray cinder cone rising from the bottom far below. Why, the crater was as deep as streets of the City of Helam were long! Steam clouds churned out of fissures in pools of congealed melted rock near the small cone in the bottom. Esther thought it was a fearful sight, as if the jaws of hell gaped open to receive her. She drew back from the edge. Alma put his arm around her and guided her to a spot where she could sit down.

There was absolute silence except for the chugging of hot rock and steam. She held on tightly to Alma's hand. What she had seen unsettled her. She sat there, listening to the rushing wind, recovering from dizziness brought on by looking down into the crater.

Descending was much quicker than the uphill climb had been. As they neared the forest, they crossed a big tongue of lava which lay across a small valley, damming a pool of water which reflected the buttermilk sky. Muddy edges were dotted and pressed with hoofprints and pawprints of a multitude of animals. Thickly blossoming red bougainvillaea cascaded over lava upthrusts.

Esther and Alma rested on lava rocks while Zoram played warrior with a broken staff and Netta and Leesa chased butterflies through the small meadow.

Esther could feel the intensity of Alma's thoughts. She queried, "Why was it so important we climb the volcano?"

Alma took a few moments to respond. Then he looked at her, his eyes misting. "We all need solid memories to hold to when problems come. Today we were building memories. From now on, whenever Zoram sees Tanza, he will look at it proudly and say to himself, 'I climbed that with my father.' The memory will become a source of strength to him."

Esther nodded. "Yes. My father once said the memories we build of summer flowers carries on even when the flowers are gone."

"Your father was a wise man."

Esther threw back her head and closed her eyes, trying to relax the tension of tired muscles.

Zoram returned, panting, holding an armored grasshopper which was the orange-red color of seasoned mahogany. He sat on the rock beside his father. Alma put his arm around him.

"My son," he said. "I have hunted often in this place." He roughened Zoram's hair. "Would you and Bones like to come hunting here with me?"

"Yes, we would," Zoram replied, releasing the grasshopper and watching its erratic flight.

Esther felt her heart swell within her breast. She lay back on the warm rock, feeling satisfied with her life. She closed her eyes, sniffing afternoon scents the canyon breeze brought to them: sun-warmed pine and damp earth, meadow flowers, even a hint of mint. A shadow passed over her. She opened her eyes and watched the cloudbank riding the west wind as it bisected the landscape with its shadow.

Then she felt slight movement within her womb and smiled inwardly. She had kept her secret well. She was building some of her own strong memories.

* * *

For most of his life, Alma had been fairly sure of himself, but each time Esther approached her confinement he seemed to become more nervous. He thought how easy it would be to go hunting and come back after the baby was born. But such an escape wouldn't be fair to himself or to Esther. She was so moody. She wanted this and that and something else. He smiled. But I'm not complaining, he thought. She's the one in misery. He hadn't been home during Zoram's birth, but was away doing something for King Noah. As each of the girls came into the world, he had been by Esther's side.

Now, as this new baby's birth approached, Esther again implored with her eyes that he stay near. The room's heat was oppressive. Seeing Esther resting, he quietly slipped out. He stepped into the night and thankfully breathed the cool air. He stretched his arms, then his entire body.

The lake was a sheet of bronze before him, holding and reflecting rays of the half-moon. Images of torches from the village danced low on the water. The night held lake scents, acrid woodsmoke and pine, and the smell of rain. He looked again at the sky. Westward, boiling over Tanza, storm-clouds piled one atop the other, seeming to battle for the right to sweep into the little valley. Dark clouds brushed the tops of mountains, and where the moon had been bright, land now became as black as the inside of a cave.

Then came thunder, booming and rolling, shaking the very earth. Drops of rain as big as berries hit him on his bare chest and head. He breathed deeply of the stormy night. The sky was suddenly rent with sheets of white lightning which lit up the black land and seemed to split the volcanoes themselves. He sighed and walked slowly back into his house.

* * *

The baby was a dark-haired look-alike of his father. Alma sat by Esther's bedside, watching lovingly as the midwife placed the swaddled baby in Esther's arms. She held him close, then apparently noticing Alma's outstretched hands, carefully placed the small bundle in them. Alma held him proudly, walking around with the baby held high. Sitting down again, he leaned back and studied the tiny red-wrinkled face. He felt Esther's touch and took her hand in his, then kissed her fingertips while still holding the baby. Clearing his throat, he broke the almost-magic silence.

"His name shall be as mine," he said. "We shall call him Alma. He will carry on the priesthood leadership."

* * *

Alma stooped over and pulled a thistle from the ground. As he worked his way down the row of corn, his mind drifted back over the twenty-four years since he led his people from the Land of Lehi-Nephi. Time had passed so quickly. When they left the Waters of Mormon there were only about four hundred people. Now more than two thousand lived in Helam.

Zoram had been five when they arrived in this valley. Now, at twenty-eight, he stood a head taller than his father. He had married Micael, Helam's oldest daughter. During the past year Micael had presented Alma and Esther with their first granddaughter, beautiful brown-haired Ma'Loni. Zoram's red hair and bushy red eyebrows, which almost met above his eyes, gave him a look of fierceness. His nose was large like his father's, and his chin was hard and firm. Alma looked at him now. Zoram really had a look of power about him as he hoed the ground next to his father.

With his training as a scribe, Zoram often helped Alma with his records, but Alma knew his son's interest was in the out-of-doors. Hunting and fishing and warrior training were his great loves. Alma smiled as he hoed. There was no need for warriors. Helam was a land of peace. He sighed contentedly.

Alma looked to where Esther sat in the shade of a ceiba tree. She was holding little Ma'Loni while knitting some clothes. Micael and the girls sat near her. He looked at his daughters with pride. Netta was a quiet and serious twenty-two-year-old, Leesa an eighteen-year-old tomboy. Then there was their youngest. Alma's breast swelled. He allowed himself to grin. At eleven, young Alma was almost as big as a man, though right now he was stuffing his mouth with handfuls of berries and licking fingers which dripped red juices. Beside him on the ground lay his dog, the very image of Bones. The puppy had been Zoram's gift on young Alma's first birthday and was named Noah. Bones had died shortly after the puppy was born. Zoram and Alma buried him with full honors as befitting a lifelong friend.

Alma shook his head. Here I am blessed with sons I wanted, and yet . . . he looked down at the ground and continued hoeing. And yet, I am not close to my youngest son.

He vigorously attacked some weeds, taking out his keen frustration. He thought, I wonder if it is the friends he spends so much time with; especially Nehor who is nothing but a troublemaker.

He sighed, then looked upwards in gratitude as he silently praised God. The Lord had blessed him with a good home, a lovely wife, choice children, a grandchild, a covenant people, and a delightsome place in which to live. What more could he desire? With the exception of his concern about young Alma, he and his people were at peace with the world.

Alma leaned on his hoe, sweat rolling from his sun-darkened skin. He looked with pride on his straight rows of corn and sweet potatoes. His squash plants were large, and already he had picked some tender, young golden squash to be boiled.

As he again chopped at the weeds, his attention was distracted by someone running towards him. Balzar dropped out-of-breath at Alma's feet, panting as he looked up at him. His eyes rolled in fear.

"Lamanites! They have found us."

Chapter 6

The Lamanites

Thin sunshine glinted from the drawn swords of the cordon of Lamanites standing impassively between city and lake. Alma's people huddled in the city in frightened groups.

"We must arm everyone possible," Helam said, as he and Alma met to plan their strategy.

"With what?" Alma replied.

"With swords, hoes, or whatever we have with which to protect themselves."

Alma shook his head. "We have no trained army and very few weapons." He gestured towards the lake. "Those Lamanites have fought for years and are well-armed. Without training and adequate weapons, our people will be slaughtered. Are you prepared to accept responsibility for hundreds of deaths?"

Helam walked to the stool and sat down, his head bowed. When he looked up his face showed distress. "We can't meekly surrender to them. They'll make us slaves, abuse our women, and kill everyone anyway."

"What alternatives do we have?" Alma asked quietly. "I value my freedom as much as you or anyone else values freedom, but I also value my life and the lives of our people."

"Then you think we should surrender without a fight?"

"Helam, at this time I see no alternative but to trust God's goodness."

Helam sighed. "So be it. We must tell the people." As he walked away, he muttered, "I hope we won't have occasion to regret this decision."

They separated, going from group to group, calming the people—reminding them that they were the Lord's people and He would protect them.

Gathered in the square before the temple was the largest group. Alma climbed the steps. Standing above the people, he shouted to them.

"Why do you fear? The Lord brought us here and has protected us for these many years. Our faith has never been tested since leaving the Land of Nephi. In this present affliction, let us be strong. Put your trust in the Lord. Pray that the hearts of the Lamanites might be softened and that they will leave us in peace."

A soft rustling of clothing was heard as the people knelt on hard-packed earth. Heads bowed in supplication and the rhythmic sound of hundreds of voices rose in prayer.

Alma offered his own prayer of faith, then joined Helam. Side by side they stepped out to meet the Lamanite army. Clouds overhead thickened, dulling the gray light of afternoon. As the soaking drizzle started to fall, Alma and Helam walked towards where the Lamanite leader stood.

Alma had shouted for his people to have faith and to not worry, but as he and Helam strode towards the Lamanites he anguished in his mind. For over twenty-five years we have lived in peace, he reasoned. Now what will happen to us? The Lord has promised me that our people will not be killed, so will we be as Joseph's descendants in Egypt: slaves? Or will the Lord prevent the Lamanites from capturing the land of Helam? "Whatever Thou wilt, O Lord," he whispered.

"What was that," came Helam's voice.

Alma looked sadly at his friend and shook his head, continuing with his thoughts. He looked at the sky and thought back over his life. Had there been any time since his conversion that he had not been faithful to his covenants? No. He could not think of anything he might have done to displease God. He sighed, then caught himself. Here I have challenged the people to trust the Lord and yet I am questioning. Forgive me, Father, he said silently. What will be, will be. My life, and the lives of my people, are in Thy hands.

Words came into his mind. *I am ever with you, my son.*

He and Helam were nearing the massed ranks of dark-skinned warriors. The Lamanites, armed with spears and swords, were naked except for leather sandals and an animal skin loincloth topped with leather sword belt. Bronze bodies glistened in the rain, almost as if they had been rubbed with animal fat. They were tall, handsome, beardless men, their hair blue-black in color.

One whom Alma surmised was the Lamanite leader stood in front of his army, leaning on a heavy staff, watching their approach. A beautifully spotted ocelot fur was draped over his right shoulder. Alma noted that though he appeared older than most of the warriors, the Lamanite's body was muscular and trim. His brows were heavy, hiding his eyes. His graying hair was cropped close to his head.

Alma stopped a half-pace behind Helam.

"Welcome to the Land of Helam. I am Helam, leader of this people. What is it you desire in our land?"

For several moments the Lamanite leader looked them over, from head-dress to sandals.

"I am Laman, king of Shilom and Shemlon." Then with admiration he continued. "This is a great city." A look of cunning narrowed his eyes.

"We want to leave you in peace. We need directions to help us return to our own land."

Alma stepped forward. "You will leave us in peace if we give such directions?"

"Yes. We are a peaceful people. Just give us directions to the Land of Shemlon and we will leave you."

Alma, still suspicious of the King, noted that Helam looked relieved. Motioning to King Laman, Helam dropped to one knee. He smoothed the sand in a wide arc before him, then began to painstakingly draw a map, showing the present location of the Lamanites and the valley to follow for their return to the Land of Nephi.

Alma watched, an uneasy feeling in his stomach. Then he started in surprise. Coming up behind the Lamanite king was a Nephite! The Nephite's tunic and cape were soft jaguar skins, and on his head was a headdress resplendent with iridescent blue-green plumes of the quetzal bird. Though it had been twenty-five years, Alma recognized the man: Amulon, chief priest for King Noah! Alma felt helpless dismay.

Helam and the Lamanite king stood. Amulon stepped forward, bowed dutifully before King Laman, then turned to Alma and Helam, a crooked grin on his face.

"So," he said, nodding his head, "this is where the errant priests have disappeared to."

Laman wiped his hands on his fur, then motioned several warriors forward.

"Amulon, I am assigning you to stay here and govern this land. I will leave warriors to guard the people."

"But . . . " Helam started to protest.

Laman silenced him with a curt gesture. "Did you think I would be so foolish as to let you live here without our protection?" he asked. His question was followed by a loud guffaw. He slapped Amulon on the back, enjoying his little joke.

Amulon smiled coldly.

Helam's eyes hardened. "So, you still believe in treachery?"

Without answer, Amulon struck Helam across the face. Helam's fists doubled but he restrained his anger. He ignored Amulon and faced King Laman.

"We ask you to honor your promise and leave our land," he said coldly. "We are a peaceful people. We want neither your presence nor your protection."

King Laman only grinned more widely. "I have appointed Amulon to be king and ruler over this people. He and his fellow Nephites will govern you and give your people the security they deserve."

Alma looked Amulon in the eyes, "If we give up our liberty for security, we deserve neither liberty nor security."

"Still one to make high-sounding speeches, eh?" Amulon said harshly. "Enough talk. We must have houses to live in. Your house, Alma, shall be mine. See what effect your flowery words have on that decision. We will also need seven additional houses in which to quarter your governing priests." He pointed a finger at Helam. "Your house will be used for the Lamanite guards.

"Now, go. Remove your things and prepare your homes for our occupation."

Alma took the seething Helam by the arm, turning him towards the city. They were silent most of the way back. Then Alma felt a tremor go through Helam.

"They cannot do this. We will take arms and expulse them from our land."

Putting his hand on Helam's arm, Alma said sadly, "My friend, I have similar feelings. We have been betrayed, but as I said before, our people are not trained in arms. Few even own a sword. Many would be killed. It is better that we submit peaceably at this time." He shrugged. "Later? . . . "

* * *

Esther stood on her porch watching for Alma's return. Zoram stood behind her in the doorway, a partially-concealed sword in his hand. Micael and the other children remained inside. Esther looked around for young Alma, but he and his dog were not to be seen.

As Alma came down the street, Esther knew something was wrong just by the way he walked. He waved to her as he approached, then as he hugged her she felt the tenseness of his body.

"What has happened, my husband?" she asked, watching his eyes.

"The Lamanites have put us under their custody," he said. Then he shook his head. "But that is not the worst part. We are to be governed by the priests of Noah, led by the wicked Amulon."

Her hand went involuntarily to her mouth and she drew back. "But how . . . ?"

Alma shrugged. "I don't know why Amulon and his priests are with the Lamanites. But they are. And . . . " his voice dropped, as with embarrassment.

"And what?"

Alma was not usually at a loss for words, but Esther could see he was really troubled. He shrugged with resignation. "Amulon has demanded our house as his place to live."

"Our house?" Then the full impact of his words were clear. "But where . . . ?"

Zoram stepped forward, his eyes burning. "No one else will live in our house." He assumed a militant pose on the porch, his sword across his chest.

Esther turned to him soberly, her hand on his wrist. "No, my son." Shaking her head, she continued, "We have lived in a tent before. We can do it again."

Ignoring Zoram's protests, she returned her attention to Alma. "But what of the rest of the people? What will happen to them?"

Alma shook his head sadly. "We must provide quarters for the priests and all of the Lamanite guards. Helam and his family are also required to vacate their house."

"Oh, no." Esther spoke with compassion. "Annah is ill. Even with the help of their older girls, it will be a real hardship for her."

Shedding tears over the house and the things she was forced to leave behind, Esther rolled the family's personal things in blankets while Alma and Zoram set up their tent on the edge of the forest. She looked back sadly as she left her home. Would she ever live in it again? What of all the furniture which Alma had lovingly made for them?

* * *

Alma had his own concerns. Where was young Alma? An eleven-year-old should not be roaming around the city. Especially when we don't know how vicious these Lamanites might be. He didn't say anything, though, as he didn't want Esther to worry unnecessarily. She seemed worried enough as it was.

He had one other concern. What of the sacred records? If Amulon discovered them they would be destroyed or confiscated. While Zoram took charge of setting up the tent and moving what furniture Amulon permitted them to take, Alma slipped off into the woods, his arms filled with scrolls and papers. There was a hollow tree close to his little glen in the forest. He went there now, carefully storing the records against any rain. When he was satisfied the scrolls could not be seen he returned to the village. He would find a better place for them when he could.

Young Alma finally showed up at sundown, faithful dog trotting behind. He walked into the almost empty house, a perplexed look on his face.

"Come here," Alma said, his voice flat and expressionless. "Come here and stand beside me and tell me where you have been all day."

His son grinned mischievously. "Nehor and I and several other boys fixed us a hideout where we can keep out of sight of the Lamanites."

"Do you think we don't worry about you when you are gone?"

"But father," he hung his head and gritted his teeth, as if to say, What's the use?

"Besides," Alma continued. "I don't like you hanging around with young Nehor. He is not a good influence on you."

"Nehor's all right." He looked around again, as if noticing for the first time that most of the furniture had been moved from the house. "What's happening?" He appeared anxious to change the subject.

Alma shrugged. "Amulon has ordered us out of our house. We are going to be living in our tent."

Young Alma bristled. "You just let him tell you to move out?" He shook his head in disbelief. "You didn't fight him or anything?"

Alma shook his head sadly. "No, I didn't fight him. There was nothing I could do." He grasped his son's shoulders. "As for you, since you were not home to help move our furniture and possessions, please hurry to Helam's house and help his family move."

His eyes big, young Alma asked, "Is Helam's family moving, too?"

Alma nodded affirmatively. He watched as Alma turned to the door. He lifted his arm as if to put it around young Alma's shoulders, but before he touched him he dropped it back to his side in frustration. He could tell that his son was disappointed in him.

* * *

Darkness had fallen by the time everything was moved to the tents. They had worked hard, but for the youthful Alma it had been exciting. Shyly he turned to Ruth, Helam's youngest daughter.

"Shall we go to the lake and wash?"

She smiled at him and nodded.

Alma held her hand as they walked through the village. He fixed his eyes straight ahead, studiously ignoring Lamanite guards standing on corners. A chill breeze was blowing as they approached the lake. Ignoring it, and still holding Ruth's hand, Alma ran into the water. Shouting merrily, they splashed each other until both were soaking wet. Noah stood on the beach and barked at them. Alma sat down in the water, cupping water in his hands and pouring it over his head. Cold water really felt good on his hot body. Dripping wet, they emerged from the water and trudged back to their tents. He glanced over at Ruth. Her wet dress clung tightly to her young body. Alma felt a stirring within. He smiled as he and Ruth and his dog made their way to the tents.

* * *

Sometimes, as Alma looked at the servitude of his people, he wished he had armed them and fortified their city. Maybe Zoram was right; perhaps arms were necessary. Each day his heart ached as he saw people whipped, beaten, and forced to carry heavy burdens. Everything his people produced was subjected to a heavy tax by the Lamanites. He gained greater insight into problems faced by the Children of Israel while they were slaves in Egypt.

As often as he could sneak away, he went into the forest to his lonely glade and cried, "Lord, send a Moses to this people. Free us of our slavery." Only the echo of his own voice answered him.

During the days, his sons, Zoram and young Alma, worked beside him. One day, as they were working in the forest, gathering firewood for the homes of the priests, Alma noticed a tree which brought back memories of similar trees in forests near the land of his childhood.

"My sons," he called. "Come here. Notice this tree."

Zoram, whose mind was most often filled with ways he could fight the Lamanites, looked up at the huge tree covered with flaming red flowers.

"The tree is called the strangler fig," Alma said as young Alma continued to gather sticks from around it. "A few years ago it started as a small vine high in a tree. Small sprouts and roots emerged from the vine which then crept over the branches of the tree, continuing to grow down and around the trunk until they finally reached the ground."

He pointed out the sinuous trunk. "After rooting firmly in the ground, stems and shoots continued to grow and wind around the trunk of the host tree, eventually choking it to death. By this time the strangler fig which you see is rooted in the ground and has its own branches." He kicked at what was left of the host tree, knocking rotted material onto the ground.

Young Alma looked at him quizzically, apparently not understanding.

"Sons, our people are like the host tree. Amulon, his wicked priests, and the Lamanites are the strangler fig. I'm afraid if we let them dominate us long enough we will die and rot away."

Understanding gleamed in Zoram's eyes. This was language he understood. "Then we must rid ourselves of the priests and Lamanites before it is too late."

Alma smiled. "The Lord will direct us in His own time."

"Why not now?"

"I have prayed for such deliverance."

"Has the Lord answered your prayers?"

"Not yet. But I found out a long time ago, when the Lord doesn't answer our prayers, it is because He has other plans for us."

Zoram frowned. Alma knew his oldest son wanted immediate action. More difficult for him to understand was the look in young Alma's eyes. Oh, but he wished he were closer to his youngest son. Since the Lamanites came to Helam, his relationship with young Alma had drifted even further apart. There seemed to be little communication between them.

* * *

Several Lamanite guards and priests were friendly to Alma. One guard was especially cheerful, greeting Alma with a smile each time he passed. Often Alma would stop to chat. The Lamanite warrior's name was Malkish. He seemed very lonely and Alma often invited him to their tent for a meal and visit. Each time Malkish came, young Alma would quickly leave. This saddened Alma.

When Malkish's wife and little girl arrived from the Land of Shemlon, Alma and Esther invited them for dinner of peccary and vegetables. Malkish's wife was named Arina, the daughter, Abish. Arina was shy, but she seemed to listen intently as Alma and Malkish discussed their differing philosophies of life. Alma could see that both Malkish and Arina were interested in religion. He spoke often of the words of Abinadi and his own conversion.

Alma was also surprised when he realized that all of Amulon's priests had Lamanite wives. In the days when he was also one of Noah's priests, they all had Nephite wives and concubines. He was puzzled.

One day, as he worked in the fields, Tay, one of the priests who had been friendly to him when he was in the service of Noah, came and stood near him. Alma could tell Tay wanted to talk, so he finally asked the question troubling him.

"Tell me, Tay, how it is you and the other priests became involved with the Lamanites?"

At first, Tay seemed reluctant to discuss that particular subject, but then he began the story.

"After you and your people left the City of Nephi, Noah sent his army to find you and slay all of you."

Alma smiled wryly. "Yes, I was aware of that."

"When the army returned empty-handed, the king was furious. He removed the general in charge of the army and had him beheaded. The general was very popular with the people and his death caused great contention. Noah's life was threatened so he increased reprisals." He shrugged. "I suppose you can guess what that led to?"

Alma smiled knowingly. "Yes, I imagine the rebellion of the people increased."

"Yes. In fact, one of the soldiers, a man by the name of Gideon, actually fought with the king. Noah hid himself in the tower of Shilom."

Alma nodded. He remembered Gideon, a huge warrior and man of valor.

"Gideon would have killed him right then, but as they were fighting the king saw Lamanite armies approaching and called upon Gideon's patriotism for unity against the Lamanites."

"I am sure he was more concerned about his own life."

"That's true. Instead of staying to fight the Lamanites, the king urged everyone to flee into the wilderness."

Alma suggested wryly, "And I suppose Noah, fat as he was, was right in front."

Tay hung his head. "Yes, but so were many of us. We were very frightened. We were running for our lives."

"So you abandoned the City of Nephi?"

"Yes. Everyone left that could walk or run. But the Lamanites were not encumbered with women and children so they moved much faster than we could. They soon caught up with us."

Alma noticed the flush of embarrassment on Tay's face. He asked gently, "Then what happened?"

Tay seemed hesitant to go on. He looked at the ground as he continued. "Noah commanded us to leave our wives and children and escape from the Lamanites."

Air expelled from Alma's lungs in a whoosh. Leave their women and children? A cowardly act!

Tay looked at the ground as he continued. "Some men stayed behind but the rest of us ran for the deep forest."

Alma was silent, understanding Tay's embarrassment and shame at the actions of the king and those who had deserted their families to certain death.

"When the men were hidden deep in the forest, safe from the Lamanites," Tay continued, now seemingly anxious to talk, "we suddenly realized what we had done. Our guilt was heavy to bear. Several started back, saying they would rather perish with their wives and children than live as cowards in the wilderness."

Good for them, Alma applauded silently.

"But King Noah forbade them to leave. He needed all of the men to fight for him in case the Lamanites found them."

"And?" Alma's hoeing was now forgotten.

"A strong man, Gershon by name, stood angrily before the men. He rallied the dissenters around him, challenging them by memory of their wives and children to unite against the king." He paused.

Alma could see the anguish on his face.

"I wish now I had made the decision to join with Gershon," Tay said softly, then glanced around to make sure no one heard his mutinous words.

Alma knew some of the feelings that were going on inside Tay's head. He had been faced with life-changing decisions himself. He remembered the words of wisdom his father taught him: "When the time for decision arrives, the time of preparation is past."

As he remembered the scene, Tay continued. "They caught the king and tied him to a huge, dead pine tree." He shuddered. "Then they set it afire. His cries of anguish were awful."

Alma could not help remarking, "So, Abinadi's prophecy did come true?"

"Abinadi's prophecy?"

"Yes, his words just before he died were 'Yea, and ye shall be smitten on every hand, and shall be driven and scattered to and fro, even as a wild flock is driven by wild and ferocious beasts. And in that day ye shall be taken by the hand of your enemies, and then ye shall suffer, as I suffer, the pains of death by fire."

Tay's face blanched as white as the clouds which laced the sky overhead. "I had forgotten those words," he said softly as he remembered what he and the other priests did to the prophet.

"And after Noah's death?" Alma prompted.

"Then Gershon and his men attempted to put us to death, but we escaped." He again paused, perhaps thinking of their plight, without supplies in the depths of the forest—fearing death from the animals of the forest, but fearing their angry people more.

Alma waited patiently for Tay to finish the story.

"Amulon took over the leadership and directed us to stay close to the Land of Nephi, so we could steal food from the gardens of the people."

Alma interrupted, surprise in his voice. "You mean the people weren't all slain by the Lamanites?"

"No, the Lamanites captured them and returned to the city. Now we were the outcasts. For several months we scrounged for food and clothing. We stole grain and whatever else we could. We missed our own wives and children greatly, but we did not dare return. We feared the people would kill us." He shrugged eloquently as he looked at Alma, "What were we to do?

"One day, as we foraged near the Land of Shemlon hoping to find clothing to replace our tattered rags, we heard singing. We crept up close to a clearing. Several hundred Lamanite girls and women were dancing and singing." His eyes lighted as he thought of the experience. "Quite a celebration."

"Well, we waited and watched them until most left; then ran out and captured some to be our wives."

"Didn't the Lamanites chase you for stealing their daughters?"

"No," Tay said proudly. "Only twenty-four girls were left. We captured them all. No one was left to tell the Lamanites what happened. I'm sure the people of the Land of Nephi were blamed."

Tay stopped, as if he were finished.

"Is that all?"

Tay shrugged. "Just about. We left the Land of Nephi and wandered in the wilderness until we found a valley where we lived with our new wives. We did like you did here." He waved towards the city with his arm. "We built houses and were quite comfortable until Laman and his Lamanites found us."

"How did that happen?"

"Oh, the Lamanite army had been chasing King Limhi and his people who escaped from the Land of Nephi. The Lamanites became lost and stumbled upon our valley, the land of Amulon." He picked a stalk of corn and chewed on it as he talked. "They would have killed us, but Amulon sent out our wives—their Lamanite daughters—and our children to plead for our lives. They spared us and we were on our way back to the Land of Nephi when we stumbled upon your city. Pretty lucky, huh?"

After Tay left, Alma reviewed what he had said. So Limhi and his people escaped from the Land of Nephi. Alma thought of his cousin, Limhi. They were about the same age. He hoped Limhi had been able to take his people back to the City of Zarahemla which their forefathers had left almost a hundred years before. Oh, that he and his people could also escape!

He leaned on his hoe and uttered a prayer. "Father, we have borne the burdens willingly that Amulon and his people have placed upon us. Please free us from bondage." He looked up expectantly at the empty gray heavens above him.

Another surprise awaited Alma when he returned to his tent. Malkish, the Lamanite guard, was there with his wife and daughter. Esther had a rosy glow in her cheeks, her eyes were misty wet. Young Alma was not around.

Malkish stepped forward and greeted Alma. "We have a great favor to ask of you," Malkish said. "We desire to be baptized into your faith."

"Baptized?" Alma was surprised.

"Yes," Malkish hurried on. "We have been ordered back to the land of Shemlon. Before we leave we want to be baptized."

Knowing the pressures this righteous Lamanite family would suffer if their conversion were known, Alma baptized them in the nighttime so no one else would know. Baptism was a special experience for them, as well as for him. Malkish, Arina, and Abish were his first Lamanite converts. Before they departed for the land of Shemlon, Alma gave each of them a blessing. Without understanding why, he felt inspired to say as he blessed young Abish, "You will play an important part in the conversion of your people."

Chapter 7

Exodus Two

Gritting his teeth, shoulders bent, Alma toted the load of rocks up the hill. A tumpline, taut against his forehead, helped balance the load, but he still felt as if his legs were driving into the soft dirt. His back ached as if it would break. His left knee began to buckle. By sheer will he kept moving up the trail. He had made up his mind he would not complain although there were numerous things to complain about.

Through the months and years of their captivity it was Alma who bore the brunt of Amulon's anger. The Lamanites took the other priests back to the lands of Nephi, Shemlon and Shilom. Only Amulon remained, and it seemed that each day he became more vindictive against Alma. Under Amulon's direction, the guards spent most of their time harrassing Alma's people and extracting taxes to be sent back to Shemlon.

One of Alma's primary concerns was how his people would be able to continue feeding the Lamanites who were left as guards—guards whose wives and children had joined them, thus creating an even larger group to be fed and housed.

Alma looked back over the three years that he and his people had served as slaves to the Lamanites. His sons, Zoram and young Alma, were his greatest problems. At thirty, Zoram was strong and strong-willed. His greatest desire was to organize men of the community to war against their oppressors. Alma was thankful Zoram would still listen to reason.

"But why do we allow ourselves to remain as slaves to these Lamanite masters?" was Zoram's most oft-repeated question.

"I don't know," Alma replied. "The Lord hasn't told me. But I do know He will protect us. In my own mind I feel the Lord wants to bless us, but I also feel He will never give a people superior blessings without severe trials to prove them. It has not been easy to see our freedom disappear, our people beaten, our homes confiscated and turned into barracks. I haven't enjoyed becoming a beast of burden. Yet, through all of this, I believe this trial will prove whether we are worthy of blessings."

"But why must we be tried?"

"My son, I believe the greater our opportunities, the greater the obstacles the enemy will create for us. This is a time for proving ourselves."

Alma thought of an example which might help Zoram. "When I was a child in the land of Nephi, our family had chickens. Often, while gathering eggs I watched the eggs which were about to hatch. One day, after scaring off the setting hen, I saw several chicks had already hatched. I was excited and ready to go tell my father, when I noticed that two chicks had barely pecked through their shells. The eggs rolled with their struggle as they attempted to peck free. I wanted to be helpful, so I peeled off egg shells and set them free. Can you guess what happened?"

"No."

"The chicks which pecked free by themselves were healthy and lived. Those which I helped, died."

"I still don't see the significance."

"My son, it is part of life that we struggle in order to be strong. Chicks needed to struggle out of their shells to have strength and vitality to live. We, too, need to struggle. We need to fail and learn to overcome defeat. Through our struggles we will become a strong self-reliant people able to further the work of the Lord. Without strength gained from struggle, the first wind of adversity would blow us over and we would perish."

Zoram seemed, finally, to understand. "But what can we do?"

"We can listen and wait. The Lord will tell us when the time comes to overthrow the yoke of the Lamanites."

"Listen and wait? For what? You showed me the strangler fig. We are being strangled. Right now, with luck, we could capture the arms of the Lamanites, kill them, and . . . "

Alma interrupted his impetuous son. "Zoram, someday you will be a great leader. Now is not the time for swords. As difficult as waiting is we must wait." He shrugged helplessly. "And right now, that is all we can do: just wait and listen."

Though Zoram, headstrong as he was, could be reasoned with, Alma was aware that young Alma, on the other hand, was taking matters into his own hands. He was barely fourteen, but he, Nehor, and some of young Alma's ruffian friends involved themselves in numerous depredations against the Lamanites and Amulon. Officially, no one knew who stole swords from the storehouse, or threw rotten birds' eggs at Amulon's house, or dropped sleeping guards' sandals into the latrine. The Lamanites were incensed when their feather flags and standards were stolen, later to be found in a goat pen.

Several times Alma attempted to talk with his son to discourage such actions. He felt as if he were talking to a wall of his tent. Young Alma had a way of tilting his head back and looking above his head, pretending to listen, but not really hearing a word.

One evening while Alma was writing, young Alma ran breathlessly into the tent. "Father! Father!"

Alma rose and turned to meet his obviously distraught son.

"They have taken Ruth!" young Alma cried breathlessly.

"What?" Alma replied. He knew young Alma's feelings toward Helam's youngest daughter.

"Amulon and the Lamanites. They have taken Ruth."

"But why?" Alma shook his head. "Why would they take Ruth? She is but a girl."

Before his son could answer, Helam slumped into the tent, his face a map of sorrow, his white hair in disarray.

"Have you heard?" he asked dejectedly.

"Alma just told me Ruth has been kidnapped by the Lamanites. Helam, what has happened?"

Helam bit his lip and struggled to control his emotions.

"Amulon and several Lamanite guards came to our tent. They forced their way inside and grabbed Ruth. I...I tried to stop them, but they just pushed me down." He looked imploringly at Alma. "Alma, what can we do? They have Ruth. I'm afraid of what they will do with her."

Alma put his arm around his friend. "This is a shock to me," he said. "I don't know what happened but I intend to find out."

Helam sat down, his head in his hands. He looked up at Alma. "Oh, why did I let you talk me into not fighting. We should have resisted the Lamanites the day they came into our valley."

From the corner of his eye, Alma saw young Alma nod vigorously in assent.

Leaving Helam and his family behind, Alma strode quickly to his old home—the home where Amulon now lived. He banged on the pine door until a Lamanite servant, candle in hand, appeared.

"I must see Amulon."

"He is not here."

"It is imperative that I see him!" Alma shouted. "Where is he?"

"He went to the temple . . . "

Alma didn't hear the rest of the servant's sentence. He was on his way to the stone temple in the center of the city.

The plaza before the temple was brightly lighted with burning torches held by dozens of Lamanite warriors. On the steps before them stood Amulon, dressed in all his feathery finery. Alma pushed through the warriors until he faced the old priest. Only then, in the hush of the square, did he hear sounds of women keening in the night air. He looked around. In the center of the circle of guards were a number of young Nephite girls. He recognized several of them, one of whom was Ruth.

Amulon looked down at him, a leer on his face. "What is it you want?"

Pointing at the girls, Alma asked, "Why have you taken these girls from their parents?"

Amulon smiled wickedly. "These young virgins have the great honor of being selected to be temple maidens in the Land of Nephi."

Alma's eyes narrowed as he looked at the evil priest before him. "These are my people," he said. "I forbid you to take any of them. Release them at once."

Amulon gestured with his hand. Alma turned to see a warrior's swinging his club at his head. He ducked, but too late.

* * *

Esther was worried. Alma had not said where he was going or when he would be returning. Helam, a sorrowful look on his face, tired of waiting and returned to his grief-stricken wife. Young Alma had also disappeared. Impatiently Esther finished mending one of Alma's tunics, then dropped it to the floor.

She could wait no longer. She threw a gray wool shawl over her head and shoulders and left the tent. As she stepped into the inky blackness she shuddered with fear, then straightened her shoulders. Her husband was in danger. She could feel it. Fears would have to wait.

No one challenged her as she passed through the north gate of the city. The streets were dark and quiet.

She stopped in front of their old home. No lights shone from the windows. Now where? she asked herself. Her feet led her to the square before the temple. Several torches still flickered before the great building. By their light she saw a crumpled form. She hurried to it. Alma! She cradled his bloody head in her lap, cooing to him as tears ran down her cheeks. Was he dead? The thought almost paralyzed her. What would she do?

A low moan came from dry lips. He was alive! She bent over and kissed him. He stirred and moaned again, louder this time. His eyes blinked, then opened.

Alma and Esther trudged slowly up the hill to their tent. Esther bathed her husband's face and head with a damp cotton rag. Alma, a determined look on his face, stood up.

"Where are you going?"

"I must tell Helam what has happened."

"But you are still weak."

"I must go."

"Then I shall go with you."

They walked together to Helam's tent. Helam said, "Young Alma is not in the tent."

Even in the darkness Alma could feel Esther tense. Fear tinged her voice. "He left soon after you did and hasn't returned."

Alma sighed. Where could the boy be?

Helam and Annah looked expectantly at Alma as he and Esther entered their tent.

"I could not free Ruth," Alma said, shaking his head sorrowfully. "They have taken Ruth and nine other young girls to the Land of Nephi. They will serve there as temple virgins." He leaned heavily on one of the tent uprights.

Helam bent down and rummaged under a stack of robes and came up with a sword.

Alma shook his head. "It is no use, my friend. They have already left."

"Then I will go after them and stop them."

Alma looked sorrowfully at Helam. "I can't blame you for wanting to try. If I were in your place I would probably do the same thing. But I have already tried to stop them. They are heavily guarded."

While he was talking, young Alma slipped into the tent. He stood quietly, listening to his father. Now he faced him, fire in his eyes.

"It is your fault Ruth and the others were taken. You are the one who kept the people from fighting and protecting their families."

Alma started to speak, but his son stepped close and pounded on his chest with clenched fists. "I hate you, I hate you," he cried. Turning, he fled from the tent, with only the sounds of his sobs remaining.

Through misty eyes Alma looked at Esther. He was speechless. Tears were streaming down Esther's face. He put his arm around her and held her tightly to him. Helam replaced his sword and sat down wearily on the pile of robes. Annah, still silent, turned and went through the partition to the rear of the tent.

* * *

Young Alma ran blindly into the dark night. His old dog, Noah, attempted to follow him, but soon gave up and returned to the tent. Alma's feet unconsciously followed the trail which skirted the city, leading southward across the meadow—the same direction the Lamanites with their youthful prisoners had taken earlier. He stumbled and ran until he was exhausted, then he sank to his knees. He looked up at the heavens. The moon had risen and loomed now overlarge in the blurring aura of its own diffused light. Near it flared the pinprick of Venus. Young Alma stared upward at the moon and its intense, tiny companion.

"God, if there is a God, hear me," he cried. "I vow before you this night that I will go to the Land of Nephi and free Ruth and the other girls." In the limpid silence he heard only the faint, crackling whirr of busy ants, and sounds of birds, toads and monkeys in the surrounding forest.

He plodded on, far into the night. After losing the Lamanites' trail and becoming unable to go further, he lay on the forest floor and slept. He dreamed of Ruth and of his brave rescue. With morning, and realization that it was all a dream, he wept. He had failed to fulfill his vow.

His face and body burned with hundreds of insect bites. When he stopped to get a drink at a stream, he noticed by his reflection that his face was splotchy and swollen. Reluctantly, he turned and started back for his father's tent. Hungry, bitten, and exhausted, he arrived back in late afternoon. Entering the tent, he looked at the floor, avoiding his father's eyes, then dropped down, putting his arms around his dog.

Alma sighed with relief. Esther dabbed at her eyes with her fingers, then hurried to her son's side and hugged him tightly. Both had been very worried.

Lifting young Alma's chin, Alma said, "My son. I know how you must feel. Ruth was very special to you."

Esther bustled around fixing something for young Alma to eat. Alma noticed with a grin that mosquito bites had not impaired his son's appetite.

After he ate, young Alma looked fiercely at his father and said through his gritted teeth, "I hate Amulon."

"I hated him, too, for awhile."

"You don't hate him now?"

"No," Alma said gently. "I don't hate Amulon. I dislike what he has done and what he stands for."

Young Alma looked at his father. Alma put his arm around him.

"My son, throughout your life remember this. Hate is a destroying emotion. Your hate cannot hurt Amulon, the one you hate. It can hurt you."

"I still hate Amulon," young Alma said sullenly. "I'll make him pay for stealing Ruth."

"No, my son. Amulon labors under his own feelings of guilt and inadequacy. He will be punished in due time."

"Who will punish him?"

"God will punish him. It is not our responsibility."

Young Alma stubbornly persisted. "Father, instead of teaching me to write, teach me to use a sword, like Zoram."

Alma placed his hand on his son's shoulder. "Right now you are feeling the need to retaliate against the Lamanites. I can understand that. At your age I would have felt the same way. But remember, my son, knowledge is power. To be able to read and write our language will give power greater than any sword. Your power will be preservation of the language of your fathers, and writing of scriptures."

"Would that power save Ruth?" the youthful Alma asked bitterly.

Alma shook his head. "Perhaps not, but that power could save a people."

That was apparently difficult for the youthful Alma to understand. He stuck out his chin, turned and walked from the tent.

As young Alma left, Alma could see he was not convinced. He shook his head in sorrow. Young Alma's rebellious tendencies really worried him. He whispered a prayer, "Father, please help me to understand my son and to help him to grow in service to thee."

He stepped to the flap of the tent, lifted it, and watched his son running towards the city. Words of the blessing he had given the younger Alma as an infant came to him.

"My son, the Lord wants me to say to you that you are one of his chosen spirits. He has a mission for you. The greatest contributions you will make may not even be known by those around you. Your purpose will be to preserve the records and teach the people. In fulfilling your assignment, you will contribute greatly to the history of this people."

Alma had felt inspired to say those words. But now . . .

His thoughts were interrupted by a cry of despair from Helam's tent. He ran there and lifted the flap. Annah, on her knees, moaned as she rocked back and forth. Alma hurried to her side.

"What is it?"

Without looking up or breaking the rhythm of her movements, she cried, "Helam! He's gone. And so is his sword."

"Oh, no!" Alma shouted. He turned and ran for the door of the tent, hurrying into the city.

Amulon received him coldly. "What is it now?" he growled.

Alma struggled for words, finally blurting, "Helam has taken his sword. He has gone after the kidnappers of his daughter."

Amulon grinned wickedly. "So, the priest now thinks he is a warrior."

"Do something!" Alma shouted, unable to continue his composure.

Amulon shrugged. "What can I do? If foolish men want to get themselves killed . . . ?" He left the thought unfinished.

Wearily, Alma returned to his tent. Esther was attempting to comfort Annah. Young Alma had still not returned. Alma knelt in his own tent.

"Father," he whispered. "Please save my friend from harm." A coldness permeated his breast and he involuntarily shivered. It was as if the Lord had said, "I'm sorry."

He shook his bowed head in sorrow. Tears dropped unnoticed on the floor of the tent.

Days came and went with no word of Helam.

Zoram, discouraged by Helam's disappearance, asked his father, "Isn't it possible for us to just refuse to do what Amulon and his henchmen tell us?"

Alma shook his head. "No, that is what Amulon wants. We must do whatever we are asked—without complaining or criticizing."

He could see Zoram was unconvinced. Alma, himself, was not now sure that what he spoke was correct. For almost thirty years he had preached peace. Now he silently prayed the Lord would help him feel the rightness of what he was doing.

* * *

Esther was concerned about her husband. She could see that Helam's disappearance, and the increased pressures imposed by Amulon, were extremely hard on Alma. He lost weight and his face showed signs of his stress. But he did not complain. Esther smiled inwardly. Alma had never been a whiner or complainer. She knew he would continue doing whatever was necessary. His faith seemed absolute; his attitude never off-duty.

She watched as people became even more burdened with difficult tasks. Every evening Alma led prayer sessions in the Nephite's temple. There the people cried mightily to the Lord for relief. No answer.

Esther's prayers were always for Alma. She asked the Lord, "How much can You expect of him? How much can he bear before he breaks?" In her mind she received an assurance of the Lord's love. *My daughter. Peace be unto thy soul. I will soon relieve the afflictions of this people. Continue to support thy husband.* She pondered these words and put them in the innermost part of her heart.

One day Alma came home very despondent—a mood that Esther knew was just not like him. He didn't say anything to her, but after living with him for over thirty years Esther knew something was wrong. She asked, "Alma, what is the matter?"

"They found Helam," he said tonelessly.

She involuntarily put her hand to her mouth and sucked in her breath. "Is he . . . ?"

He looked at her and nodded sadly. Sitting down, he put his head in his hands.

His eyes are dry of tears, Esther thought sadly. He has already cried them. "Do you want to tell me?" she asked gently as she knelt beside him.

"Lamanite guards returned from the Land of Shemlon. Amulon called me to the temple to tell me the news." He looked up at her, a deep hurt showing in his eyes. "Helam apparently followed their trail into the jungle. When he caught up with the rear guard . . . "

Alma shrugged dispondently, then whispered, "He was no warrior, untrained with the sword. The Lamanite warriors slaughtered him. Cut him to pieces. Then left him in the jungle to rot." He moaned audibly.

Esther sat silently, holding his hands. She knew the loss he was feeling. Helam had not only been Alma's best friend, but he was the one Alma always turned to for support and confirmation of his decisions. There was nothing she could say to comfort him.

"Does Annah know?" she finally asked.

He nodded. "I stopped there first." He shook his head in agony as he apparently recalled the hurt of telling the news.

"I will go to her," Esther said as she started to rise.

Alma held her hand, pulling her back down beside him. "Please stay a moment," he said. "There is something else."

Seething anger was in his tone. He leaned forward, cupping her chin in his hands. "Amulon has decreed that we must stop praying. He has placed guards throughout the city to arrest any who violate the decree. Those arrested will be put to death."

"What will you do?"

He smiled sadly. "What do you think we will do?"

"You have always said the Lord placed you here to give balance to other people's lives. Knowing you as I do, you will go out and teach the people to pray silently."

Alma pulled her to him. Tenderly he kissed her and held her close. She could feel the beating of his great heart through her thin cotton robe. The wetness of his tears stained her cheeks. For moments he held her there, then left to go back to instruct his people.

Esther hurried to the next tent. She wished that Alma had not told Annah the news. He had a tendency to be too blunt. Perhaps she could have made it easier for her friend. When she saw Annah, she attempted to hide the shock she felt at her friend's appearance. Annah's skin was as dry and lifeless as the petals of a pressed flower; her eyes red and swollen from crying. Annah looked twice her age. Words were superfluous. Esther moved quickly to Annah and folded her against her, tightly cradling her head against her cheek. She stroked Annah's hair as the sobs came.

* * *

Alma moved among the people, giving them instructions, telling them to avoid praying aloud.

When he returned to his tent it was late. He stood outside and looked at the tent, wishing in his heart he had taken time to build Esther another home. Thank goodness for her strength. She never complained about having to live in a tent. Several of the brethren indicated their willingness to help build new homes, but Amulon kept everyone so busy there had not been time. Alma stayed outside the tent, not yet ready to go in.

He slipped around the side of the tent into the forest. Clouds obscured all but a few of the stars. Alma was sure-footed as he proceeded down the familiar trail. Deep in the forest he found the glade he sought. Here he had often poured out his soul to the Lord. Here, in the past, he had received comfort and assurance.

Now, once again, he spoke to his God.

"Father, the burdens of this, Thy people, are heavy to bear. They have been uncomplaining before Thee. They have kept Thy commandments. They have borne their burdens willingly, but need relief. Please lighten their burdens, free us from the tyranny of Amulon and the Lamanites. Give us the liberty which was once ours: to govern our own lives, to speak with Thee as we desire, to worship Thee in our holy places."

He prayed until his joints were stiff and his body weary. Still he persisted, kneeling on the soft ground of the forest, reaffirming the covenants he had made with the Lord. Finally, the answer came.

Lift up your head and be of good comfort, for I know of the covenant which ye have made unto me; and I will covenant with my people and deliver them out of bondage.

I will also ease the burdens put upon your shoulders, that even you cannot feel them upon your backs, even while you are in bondage. This will I do that ye may stand as witnesses for me hereafter, and that ye may know of a surety that I, the Lord God, do visit my people in their afflictions.

Alma shouted aloud, "Praise Thee, Lord, for Thy great mercy. Praise Thee. Praise Thee."

He didn't remember returning down the forest path to his tent. He was just there. He entered, disrobed, and crawled in beside his wife. Esther sleepily rolled over, putting her arm around his neck. He lay awake for some time, hearing her soft, regular breathing, feeling her hair as it caressed his face. Peaceful sleep finally came.

At their breakfast of porridge and wheat cakes, he shared the Lord's words with his family. His voice showed his excitement.

Esther looked at him calmly, a smile on her face. "My dear husband, in my dreams last night I heard the same words."

Zoram spoke up, "As did I."

Even young Alma, his mouth stuffed with wheat cakes, seemed amenable.

Alma was amazed. Had the Lord spoken to everyone?

On the woodcutting detail where he was assigned that day, as often as he could without the guards getting upset at him, he talked with people. Each told him a similar thing. The Lord had spoken to their minds during the night. They all heard the same promise: *I will ease your burdens.* Not since the takeover by the Lamanites had there been such a joyful and happy feeling among the people.

As promised, Alma noticed people were strengthened in their bodies so that they bore their burdens with ease. He smiled his pleasure, even sometimes whistling a song between his teeth. He knew the Lamanite guards didn't know what was going on although they must have noticed that Alma's people carried every burden without complaining.

Two Lamanite warriors came to the tent for Alma, saying they had instructions to take him to Amulon.

As Alma entered, Amulon stared at him with a look of pure hatred. His breath sounded harsh. He asked many questions which Alma answered truthfully, but he could tell that Amulon was leading up to more important ones.

Amulon leaned forward, thoughtful. Brooding disquiet was heavy in the truculent stare he fixed upon Alma. "How is it your people can do all the work I have given them and still be happy?"

Alma cheerfully answered. "With God on our side, it doesn't really matter what you do to us."

Amulon angrily rose to his feet, shook his fist at Alma and shouted, "I will yet break the backs of you and your people."

Alma smiled and politely thanked Amulon for the audience.

Again that night the voice of the Lord came to him. *Be of good comfort, Alma, for on the morrow I will deliver you out of bondage. Thou shalt lead this people, and I will go with thee.*

Alma passed on his instructions the next day, making sure everyone was contacted. "As soon as it is dark, gather your flocks, your grain, and any other belongings to take with you. We will flee the Land of Helam and the oppression of Amulon and the Lamanites."

Alma was convinced that the most excited person in the city was Zoram. Family members spent all night packing the few belongings they would be able to carry. Young Alma was assigned the responsibility for their small herd of goats. While Zoram fashioned packs for each member of the family, Alma slipped off into the forest to get his writings. By dawn all was ready. Now all Alma needed was to know what stratagem the Lord would want him to use to get the people past their Lamanite guards.

Alma slipped into the city. He was astonished to see every guard asleep at his post. He smiled as he hurried to his leaders' homes. The Lord had provided the way!

Clouds of dust converged before the city as the people, their flocks and herds with them, trooped out of every gate. Alma led his people around the lake and into the east forest. Letting Zoram temporarily lead the way, he stopped and watched as thousands streamed past. They rounded the lake and many looked back for a last look at this city which had been home for almost thirty years. He noted tears on many faces, even some looks of doubt. He could understand their feelings. For some, this was the second time they had abandoned their homes and all they had worked for.

The noise, dust and commotion of thousands of people and animals tramping around the lake was intense. How could the guards sleep through it all? He hurried and caught up with his family. Zoram led the way and young Alma—old dog, Noah, on his shoulders— lagged behind with the goats. Alma placed himself beside Zoram. He thought sadly, this is where Helam should be. Since Helam's death the Lord had comforted his heart, but there was still an emptiness there. He shook the morose thoughts from him. They were leaving their home, but he knew their destiny was in the hands of the Lord. Wherever the Lord led, he and his people would follow.

All day they cut their way through the forest. Their burdens, now their own, were still light. As the sun set behind western mountains they entered a long seemingly endless valley leading towards the north. The Lord whispered to Alma, *Rest now. You are safe from your enemies.*

Swarms of tiny, white butterflies cavorted in swirling spirals above the high grass. Bees, heavy with pollen, bobbed clumsily in straight lines towards their hives. Dewed spider webs glistened like thin jewels in the fading sunlight. The pastoral scene was one of peace and harmony.

Alma directed people to pitch their tents before dark. Soon the valley looked like a tent city. Flocks and herds pastured in all directions. An open place was saved in the center of the tent area. Men and older boys dragged huge trees and branches from the forest and piled them there. Soon a great bonfire raged, casting lights and shadows on the tents, throwing showers of sparks into the night sky.

The people, except for the few who were tending flocks, gathered around the fires. There was singing and dancing; the time was one of great joy and thanksgiving. Alma led the people in anthems of praise. Their voices, it seemed to him, were as a heavenly choir, sending aloft great waves of laudation as they gave thanks to the Lord for easing their burdens, for delivering them from bondage, and for bringing them away from Amulon and his Lamanite taskmasters.

Amalakiahah quieted the crowd. "My people," he shouted, "I propose this valley be named the Valley of Alma, since it was he who led us here."

A loud shout of acclamation went up from the crowd.

Alma quieted them once again. "My friends, it is not I who has led you here, but God. He deserves the credit. Let us once again give thanks."

Chapter 8

To Zarahemla

As Alma said his private prayers that night, he thanked the Lord that once again his people slept as free men and women. When he finished, he heard a loud honking. He ran from his tent. Overhead flew a flock of wild geese, their musical cries ringing through the night, louder than he had ever heard. To him it was a sign of his people's own deliverance.

Before dawn the next morning, while Alma still lay on his blanket, the voice of the Lord once again came. *Make haste and get your people out of this land. The Lamanites have awakened and are pursuing you. Hurry on and I will stop the Lamanites in this valley that they pursue you no more.*

Alma was relieved. He trusted implicitly in the Lord, but he knew that moving several thousand people and their animals through the forest had left a huge trail for the Lamanites to follow. Even the poorest of the Lamanite trackers could follow it easily. Now he would worry no more.

Morning dawned cool and green, a morning like many others but with one exception. They were free! Dew glistened in the rays of the rising sun. Smells of dampness rose from petals and leaves. A chorus of woodpeckers rattled out robust, percussive harmony in a stand of pines. Bird life seethed in the sky. Mockingbirds sang their melodies in the meadow. Alma stood with Esther at the door of the tent, absorbing the smells and sounds. Once again the world was a world of promise for his people.

Following the course the Lord set for them, Alma led the people northward through the long valley. They forged ahead, wind in their faces and dust in their eyes. For days they meandered down the long valley of Alma. The small river became larger each day as it flowed towards the sea. Sunlit greenery along the banks of the river was so dense they had to cut their way through to get fresh water for drinking and bathing.

Game was plentiful. The river banks were replete with brightly colored frogs. Deer and wart hogs roamed the clearings near the river. Birds of every color nested in the trees. Fish slapped the water with glossy sides, rising to feed on myriad insects.

On either side of the valley were jumbled hills, valleys and occasional plateaus. As he and his people crossed dried up swamps and bogs, Alma was thankful to be traveling during the dry season. In a few months the ground would be nearly impassable.

As the refugees dropped out of the mountains and hills they saw spread before them an endless plain filled with forest and jungle. Etched against the western sky were the sharp outlines of volcanoes. Foliage changed from pine forest to a scented tangle of mahogany, sapodilla and bracken. Temperatures increased. Mosquitos swarmed, scattering like pollen out of the inhibiting undergrowth. Forests turned to jungle, became thicker and denser as they dropped to lower elevations. The sun vanished. Trees, covered with ferns, vines, bromeliads and orchids, towered high above them. Once again their progress was roofed over by sweating branches and vines. Air was now more humid; the climate so damp they could squeeze moss growing on trees and water would spray out.

Many trees were unknown to Alma. One in particular was large and stately with feathery leaves. Men knocked down the pods hanging from outlying branches and found they made excellent livestock feed.

With new things to see, new country to explore, and with children's natural exuberance, the young people seemed always in mischief. Young Alma and Nehor seemed to be the ringleaders of the boys, urging them on to see what they could do. They chased the goats; climbed trees to get at the yellow and green tree frogs resting on the leaves; threw rocks at the bats hanging upside down in the shade of the larger trees; swung in huge arcs on hanging lianas, mimicking the chattering monkeys swinging in the trees above them.

Esther was nervous about letting the boys stray too far. Several times she had seen leopards skulking through the trees. At night the wailing of jaguars sometimes kept her awake. Crocodiles had been seen in the river. There were just too many dangers around. Yet it was almost impossible to keep track of the boys all the time.

"Alma," she said. "Isn't there something we can do to keep the boys with the people? I am really concerned someone will get hurt."

"I have been worried, too," Alma replied. "But our son and his friends won't listen to me. I feel as if I am speaking to one of these trees."

Esther's and Alma's fears were realized on the evening of the eighth day after leaving Helam. Alma heard a shouting from the direction of the river. Hurrying back, he found his son's dog, Noah, disemboweled, lying beside the trail. Fear constricted his throat, making breathing difficult. Where was young Alma?

Hearing a commotion further into the forest, he ran on. Alma's friends and other curious people were clustered in a group. He pushed his way into the center. Young Alma lay on the ground, writhing and moaning. Blood ran from multiple cuts and scratches on his bare shoulders. His cheek lay open, torn flesh extending from his eye almost to his chin.

Alma knelt by his son's side, cradling his mangled head in his arms. Someone handed him a dampened cloth. He gently mopped young Alma's face, cleaning off the already congealing blood. The dampened rag brought his son to consciousness. His eyes opened. He looked directly up into Alma's eyes.

"Father," he whispered, "my body feels as if it's on fire."

Alma nodded, rocking gently back and forth, holding his son tenderly in his arms.

"Noah?" his son whispered hoarsely.

Alma shook his head.

The younger Alma closed his eyes, tears seeping from under closed lids.

"What happened?" Alma gently asked.

"I heard Noah barking," his son answered, his eyes still pressed tightly shut. "I went to see what was bothering him when I heard a hiss, almost a snake sound. I turned my head and looked right into the yellow eyes of a huge jaguar. It attacked Noah and I grabbed a stick to whack it. Before I could move it sprang at me. I could feel its breath on my face. I fell backwards, the cat on top of me. "Father, I was terrified. With both hands I held the cat's twisting head, pushing its slobbering mouth away from my face. It clawed my shoulders."

He opened eyes reddened with pain, large against the paleness of his face. "I guess I passed out."

Gently pulling young Alma into a sitting position, Alma called, "Someone get Esther." "I already sent for her," one of the men replied.

Esther pushed her way to where her husband and son were sitting. Quickly seeming to understand the situation, she knelt beside them. From her bag she drew a sweet-smelling unguent, gently dabbing it on open wounds. Then she wrapped the arm in the cool leaves of a nearby plant. Alma silently gave thanks that she had learned so much about herbs and healing.

"Are you all right?" she asked her son as she worked.

"It hurts," young Alma said.

Alma's breathing was rapid. The pulse in his temple drummed a hurried beat. How serious were young Alma's injuries? Would he live? Alma uttered a silent prayer then looked at his wife, a question in his eyes.

She shook her head.

Alma stood and motioned Zoram to him. "Find a place to set up camp," he said. "We have come far enough today."

Zoram nodded and hurried away.

Alma and several of his son's friends fashioned a stretcher from some straight limbs and strong vines. They eased the now unconscious boy onto the litter and carried him to the camp. Even after they placed young Alma in the tent, Esther refused to leave him. She swabbed the sweat from his forehead and kept fresh poultices on the open wounds. Several times when he regained consciousness for a few moments she held a gourd of water for him to drink. She gentled him when he raved.

Alma could tell how tired she was by the circles below her eyes, but she would not leave.

Alma and Nephiahah gave young Alma a blessing, promising he would be healed. Alma then stayed with Esther as long as he could, but he had a dread of seeing others suffer. He wandered through the camp, attending to the needs of his people. About every half hour he returned to his own tent and stood near his son's pallet before he turned away to resume his restless wandering.

By morning young Alma's pain and fever had eased but he was still too weak to walk. Alma organized a litter squad: young Alma's friends would take turns carrying his son down the trail.

Esther turned to him, her face tired and drawn. She looked much older than her fifty-two years. Her grey-streaked black hair was drawn back behind her head in a neat bun. Alma thought to himself that despite her exhaustion she was still a beautiful woman. He held her close, drawing to himself her gentleness, her goodness and her strength.

The lower they traveled in the valley, the worse became the insects. Flies, buzzing like mosquitoes, landed on them by the score; but they didn't bite. They seemed to like sweat. They were especially a problem on young Alma's wounds. Someone had to walk beside him just to fan away the sticky flies. Mosquitoes presented more severe problems. Alma was grateful for Esther's knowledge. She showed the people the cintronella grass, which when squeezed produced an oil which kept the mosquitoes away. Esther boiled bark of the pink-flowered tree and applied the extract to insect bites which immediately brought relief.

Despite the heat and the insects, young Alma's wounds healed fast. Soon he was limping along with friends, but his adventurous days seemed to be over.

They had been in the wilderness twelve days. That night the voice of the Lord came to Alma: *Tomorrow you will rejoin your people in the City of Zarahemla. There you will organize My Church.*

Morning light found the people up early. They emerged from the underbrush at the edge of the wide, sluggish river. Following the left bank they passed cultivated fields of corn, squash and beans. People in the fields leaned on their hoes and waved to Alma and his people as they passed.

Alma waved back. After being isolated and alone for over twenty-five years, they were again among the Nephites!

"Look," Esther whispered. He turned to look where she was pointing. Rising before them were the stone walls of a huge city.

Chapter 9

Zarahemla

Esther methodically threw the brightly wrapped shuttle back and forth through the threads of the loom. She was oblivious to the delicate pattern taking shape beneath her nimble fingers. Her thoughts were elsewhere. She was discouraged and was not sure why. She again had a home to live in; she really enjoyed Zarahemla; the people had been very kind to her. Perhaps she was just lonely.

In Helam she had become used to Alma being home every day—or at least every night. Here, after King Mosiah gave Alma permission to establish churches throughout the Land of Zarahemla, his responsibilities took him away for weeks at a time. She pouted a little. It was so unfair.

She busied herself at her loom. It was fastened high on the wall of her garden and extended to her lap. She knelt there, slamming the shuttle back and forth through the woolen fibers. As she weaved, she remembered.

* * *

It had been almost a year since Alma had led his people to Zarahemla. Fulfilling his dream, Zoram enlisted as a warrior in the army soon after their arrival. Now he served in the Land of Melek. Micael, his wife, their little girl, Ma'Loni, and their two sons, Lehi and Aha, were living in Zarahemla with Annah. At least Esther did have her grandchildren close to her.

Netta had married a childhood sweetheart named Borak and was large with child. Esther was worried about Netta. She was so tiny. Could she possibly have a baby? She wiped a tear from her eye. It didn't seem possible that her children were so grown up. Leesa had married Abelon, a stone cutter of Zarahemla. They had moved to Melek where Abelon worked in a quarry.

Young Alma still concerned her. He had recovered from the jaguar wounds without complications, but now, at almost sixteen, he really needed his father. But with Alma never home, the full responsibility of teaching and disciplining her young son had fallen upon her. It was a task she did not like. She was convinced that young Alma was not bad. He was just full of life and tended to be unruly and mischievous. She shook her head as she thought of how many times she had cried herself to sleep because of punishments she had meted out during the day.

She wondered if she was doing right by her son. He was so different from the others. Zoram and the girls had been easy to discipline. They minded her and gave her few problems. But young Alma? She questioned herself. Should Alma be punished just because he roamed the streets at night with his friends? Or just because he got into fights with the boys from Zarahemla? What should the punishment be for going into the forest by himself and not telling her where he was going? When he was a child she had relied on spanking him even though the hurt look in his eyes troubled her immensely. Now he was too big to spank. His defiant look seemed to say, I dare you to do anything.

Oh, my husband, she cried to herself. I don't know how to handle our son. Please be here to help me. But she never told him. She didn't want to distract him from his ministry.

Methodically, the shuttle raced back and forth in the loom as her mind continued to drift. Soon after arriving in Zarahemla, King Mosiah had sent out runners with a proclamation for all people to assemble. They streamed into the city from all directions, setting up shelters in the streets and in the squares. There were too many to fit in one square, so they met in several squares in the city, assembling themselves by lineage—the Nephites in one square and the people of Zarahemla in another. It was the first time all the people had assembled since the death of King Benjamin.

When they were all together on the specified day, Mosiah read to them the history of Zeniff and his people from the time they left Zarahemla until they returned. Then Limhi stood and told of his people's escape from the Lamanites. The crowd cheered and applauded.

From Alma's record, King Mosiah read of Abinadi and his words of prophecy. He read of the escape of Alma and his people from King Noah, of their lives in the Land of Helam and of their escape from the Lamanites and return to Zarahemla.

Esther noted that the story had touched many of them and they were crying. As the king read of the people escaping from the Lamanites, the people cheered in having so many people return safely to them. Then as Mosiah read of the battles, and of the wickedness of the Lamanites, the people cried again in sorrow. Young Alma had stood by her for the first part of the ceremony but then he had slipped away. She wondered where and how he had gotten the black eye which he sported. He had been reticent to even discuss it.

Esther watched with interest as wives and children of Noah's priests stepped out of the crowd. Alma had told her of the priests and their cowardly behavior of deserting their families and then kidnapping the Lamanite girls. The wives and children walked up to Mosiah, prostrating themselves before him. One stood before Mosiah to speak for the group. She was a stately woman, old, white-haired and wrinkled, but carrying herself with dignity.

"I am Mahona, once the wife of Amulon," she said simply.

King Mosiah acknowledged her with a nod.

"We," she motioned to the others, "were abandoned to certain death into the hands of the Lamanites by our husbands and fathers." She bowed before the king. "We no longer desire to be known by the names of the priests of Noah, but want to be known as Nephites. We ask that you accept our petition."

Mosiah stood and raised his hands high above his head. "Let it be known to all people," he cried, "that these wives and children who stand before me this day are now Nephites of Zarahemla, and that any bonds of marriage or family are hereby dissolved between them and their former husbands and fathers."

Esther's heart beat with pride as Mosiah then called upon Alma to speak. Alma stepped forward, standing on the platform before the people. She looked at her husband, feeling a thrill as he stood there. Though his hair was receding back from his forehead and was streaked with gray, he still held himself as erect as a young man. She smiled at his appearance. His teeth seemed large in his big warm mouth. Under his broad forehead, dark piercing eyes looked over the crowd. There were laugh-wrinkles around his eyes, setting off his large nose.

In his dramatic and far-reaching voice, Alma called upon the people to have faith in God. He told of how God had spoken to him and had led His people through the wilderness. Then he called upon the people to repent and cleanse themselves so that they could have God's power with them. Esther's eyes glistened. A tear overflowed and ran down her cheek. She hoped that her son, Alma, was where he could hear his father. She looked around, but still could not see him. Probably off with Nehor and his friends, she thought.

* * *

Even now, as she sat at the loom, her eyes became moist at the memory. I love this city, she thought. Never have I seen such grand buildings. The great temples and palaces are beautiful to behold. Helam and Nephi were beautiful places, but this! She paused in her weaving; the shuttle lay still in her hand. It would be fun, she mused, just to walk through the city, hand-in-hand with Alma. He could point out to me who lived in the fine homes, or why the temples and pyramids had been built as they had. For a moment she day-dreamed of such a walk, then almost angrily she threw the shuttle back into the loom, pulling it back and forth, back and forth.

* * *

Alma also thought often of their first year in Zarahemla. He and his people had been greeted warmly by Mosiah and his people. Alma had been immediately taken to the palace. In a long, bare room sat the king. He was a thin, young man in his thirties, bald with just a fringe of sandy-colored hair lining the sides of his head above his ears. A black mole seemed out of place above his left eyebrow. His dark brown eyes seemed to be calmly appraising Alma.

Alma bowed low from the waist. "I am Alma, a descendant of Nephi. I have brought my people from the Land of Nephi to your city. I ask that we may dwell here in peace and freedom."

The king stood and walked forward to Alma. He clasped Alma's arm firmly in his. "Limhi has told us of you. Everyone wondered what had happened to you and your people." He smiled. "I am Mosiah. I welcome you to the City of Zarahemla. I pray that it may it be a city of peace and refuge for you and your people."

"Thank you," Alma replied. "We have tents and livestock and more than two thousand people. Where do you want us to live until homes can be built?"

The king clapped his hands. Several men appeared. Mosiah gave them directions on where to settle Alma's people. All Alma heard was "in the northwestern sector of the city, towards the river."

Alma watched how people obeyed Mosiah, and how Mosiah quietly and efficiently governed. He was impressed.

After Alma's people were settled and their tents erected, Mosiah once again called him to the palace. "I want you to meet someone," he said as he greeted Alma warmly. He led him into a well-furnished sitting room behind the throne room. The room was dominated by a huge tile mosaic on one end. Alma recognized it as a picture of the tree of life—that great vision which both Lehi and Nephi had beheld.

The man who had been sitting there quickly rose and came towards them. He was a tall man with a leonine mane of hair streaked with gray. His gray eyes were wide-spaced beside an aquiline nose. His chin was strong, but soft living had given him a roll beneath his chin. Though it had been almost thirty years since he had seen him, Alma recognized him immediately. It was his cousin, Limhi, the son of Noah. They threw their arms around each other, patting each other on the back. Limhi was close to his own age, and Alma recalled how they had played warriors together as children.

During the next few days Alma and Limhi spent many hours together recounting their experiences. Limhi told him what had happened in the Land of Nephi after Alma had taken his people from the Waters of Mormon.

* * *

Limhi helped his mother through the thick underbrush. The City of Nephi lay several miles behind them. He so wished it would get dark so they could hide. He could tell how tired his mother was. Glancing around, he saw the tiredness in the movements of the other women and children. Why? he asked himself. Why had his father, the king, commanded the men to leave the women and children? It wasn't the first time in his life he was ashamed of his father, but he could not remember a time when his shame had been so strong. Not even his father's whoring around with so many concubines was as loathsome as the cowardice he had shown today.

He looked behind. There was no sign of the pursuing Lamanites, but he could hear a great thrashing in the forest behind him and an occasional scream as one of his fleeing people was cut down by Lamanite swords. He tugged on his mother's arm, but she shook her head.

"It's no use, son. I can go no further. Leave me and try to save your own life."

"No, mother. I won't leave you. If we must die, we will die together."

They emerged from the forest into a clearing. Limhi looked around at those with him. About a third of the men had refused to follow King Noah and had stayed with the women and children. They were doing just what he was doing—trying to hurry them along. Struggling through the clearing, they had almost reached the trees on the other side when a great shout was raised behind them. He looked around. Running at them from the forest was a horde of bronzed Lamanite warriors, their naked bodies glistening in the sun. Their swords, many red with blood, were raised high above their heads as they seemed to almost leap across the small meadow.

Limhi shouted to his group. "Stay. It's no use. They will be upon us before we can even get into the forest. Our only chance is to ask for mercy and hope they will listen to us."

He ran among the women and children, asking the youthful daughters to drop behind the rest and to call upon the Lamanites to have mercy and not slay them.

The rush of the Lamanites stopped as they saw the beautiful young girls and children kneeling in the grass before them. Laman, the Lamanite king, stood before his warriors. He approached the Nephite maidens, his sword hanging in his hand. He stepped up to a blonde Nephite girl, grasped her hair and pulled her to her feet. Then, without letting go, he shouted gruffly.

"Who is the leader here?"

Limhi stepped forward. "My father, Noah, is king. But . . . "

Gideon, dressed in warrior's tunic, stepped up beside Limhi. "I am Gideon, captain of Noah's palace guard. Noah, coward that he is, fled into the forest like a mole seeking his hole." He motioned towards the women and children and the remaining men. "He left his people as defenseless as a turtle on its back."

Limhi cringed at the biting sarcasm in Gideon's voice.

Pointing to Limhi, Gideon said. "This is Limhi, son of Noah. He's the rightful ruler of this people."

Laman let go of the girl's hair, shoving her aside as he strutted forward to where Limhi stood. Almost blushing at the hard scrutiny Laman gave him, Limhi stood firmly in place. Laman was as tall as he was. His body had been rubbed with animal fat until it glistened. His only clothing was a loincloth and a pair of leather sandals. The smell of his body almost made Limhi gag.

"We should kill all of you."

Limhi remained silent, looking the king in the eyes.

"We may spare you, but there are conditions. You must do what we want."

"What are your conditions?" Limhi asked suspiciously.

The king smiled wickedly. "First, you must find your father and deliver him to me. He will die at my hand."

Limhi's hands clenched and unclenched, but he continued to look at Laman.

The warrior king was still talking, "You may continue to live in your city, but you must pay one half of everything you have to my people— half your gold and silver, half your flocks and herds, half your cloth." He smiled coldly again, accenting his demands with a wave of his gory sword.

"I must confer with my people," Limhi said. He nodded with his head for Gideon to follow, then turned and retreated to where the men were standing. He repeated the demands of Laman, then commented, "We have no choice. If we don't give him what he wants, he and his warriors will kill us all. Then everything we have is theirs. As it is, we can keep half for our own use. But, more important, we will still be alive."

Gideon smiled grimly. "Alive, we always have a chance, but dead is dead. I vote for life."

The men nodded. Limhi and Gideon returned to face Laman.

"Well?" Laman sneered.

"We accept your offer."

"Good." Laman turned and motioned to his warriors. "Return them to the city," he growled loudly.

* * *

Limhi told Alma how Gideon, looking for Noah, met Gershon and the remainder of the men as they returned from the forest.

"They were repentant," he said, "and ready to face death rather than live with the knowledge of their cowardice."

He then recounted how his father, Noah, had been slain.

Alma nodded, remembering what the priest, Tay, had told him.

Then Limhi told Alma how his people had lived under the domination of the Lamanites. As Limhi told of how Laman put guards around the land, Alma nodded in understanding. He recalled the humiliation of his own people when they had been slaves to the Lamanites for only three years. Limhi's people had suffered in slavery under Laman for over twenty years.

"The priests of my father continued to trouble us," Limhi was saying. "They kidnapped the daughters of the Lamanites and carried them off into the forest."

Alma remembered again Tay's words.

"Kidnapping the Lamanite girls really caused problems," Limhi continued. "The Lamanites thought we had taken the girls and they came at us with their entire army." He smiled grimly as he remembered. "We saw them coming. Gideon deployed our own men in the forest and caught them by surprise."

* * *

Gideon was concerned. Most of the men lying in thick brush had never been in battle. They were young, inexperienced and lacked proper weapons and armor. But Gideon liked his men. They were tough, loyal and uncomplaining.

The sky above them darkened. The gray clouds turned sinister, leaving the earth in a grayness of gloom. Gideon pulled his sword a few inches from his belt, tested its honed edge, and pushed it back. He smiled with confidence. His sword was straight-bladed and ill-balanced, but it was a heavy brute of a weapon. His father had given him the sword, which he said had been patterned after the sword of Laban.

Skies seemed to open, throwing down small, spitting drops that stung his face. Thunder cracked like rumble of huge drums. Lightning slashed, piercing and blue, through the haze. Great slanting volleys of rain drowned out any human noise. The earth was drenched by seething water.

Gideon stood on a small hill, somewhat protected from the downpour by a huge pine tree. He was soaked, shivering, and made weary by the sheer weight of the water. He kept peering through the deluge, watching for the enemy. The wind billowed the rain in great scything loops, suspended it, then smashed it down even harder. It was difficult to see anything.

The worst effect of the rain, he knew, was that men's spirits seemed to sink into the earth along with the water.

There. Coming out of the forest through the clearing. The first rank of the enemy. He drew his sword and swished it through the rain. His men, seeing the signal, tensed. When the Lamanites reached the center of the meadow, Gideon waved his sword. He was thrilled to feel the weight of it in his hand after several years of boredom.

His men panting and hurried, scrambled into position, almost completely encircling the band of Lamanites. He noted that his small force was out-numbered more than two-to-one, but with the grace of God they would still beat the enemy back.

He ran down the hill, his sword held high, to meet the first of the attackers. The ambush was a complete surprise to the Lamanites. The bronzed warriors pulled their bows, but the strings were so sodden that the arrows fell short of their intended marks. Gideon could see it was going to be sword against sword.

The Nephites cheered and ran forward, their swords high. The frustration of years of subservience was suddenly vented on the enemy. They screamed defiance at those who had oppressed them.

Gideon's headlong rush brought him to the first Lamanites. He swung high his sword, slipped, and half fell in the slick mud. A rough-hewn sword stabbed at him. He hammered it to one side and kicked the man down. He saw other men falling. Screams of rage and of pain came to his ears. He strode forward, clearing his path with massive, scything blows. No Lamanite would stand and fight.

"Look to your right!" someone shouted. He turned. Lamanites were massing towards him. He waded into them, flanked on the right and left by Nephite warriors. The Lamanites jabbed at them with spears. He hacked this way and that. The flat of a sword hit him a glancing blow on the head, knocking him to his knees. He swung his sword at an enemy's legs, dodged a spear thrust, stumbled backward in the mud.

A large hand caught him. He turned to see Pahoran, one of his best lieutenants, grinning at him. "This is better than sitting on a hillside," Pahoran shouted. He held a bloodied tree limb, to use as a club.

Gideon struggled to his feet. He raised his red-dripping sword in a salute, then stepped back into the battle. Lamanites fell back before him. He climbed a small rise with Pahoran close behind. About half his men were on this side of the Lamanite force. He grinned at them, motioning with his sword. Lamanites still held the center of the meadow, but they were being pushed back towards the forest. His men attacked fiercely from all sides.

Again he raised his sword, just as enemy warriors burst upon him. He and Pahoran hurled themselves against the enemy. They yelled at the Lamanites, clubbed them with the flat sides of their swords, used captured spears. Lamanites fell before the ferocious attack, stumbled on slick mud, blinded by rain. Still Gideon and Pahoran came at them.

Gideon pushed with his sword, going for faces and throats. A heavy spear was thrust at him. He knocked it aside. The Lamanite slipped. Gideon's sword was up and falling like an axe into the man's head. The man, defenseless now, looked up in terror. Gideon tried to stop his blow. The sword swerved, thudded into mud beside his defenseless foe who looked around at his own dead, then at the big sword which had nearly killed him. Gideon saw the lips move in a thank you.

A Lamanite leader had organized a small group armed with broken spear shafts and swords, trying to hold the angry Nephites at bay. Gideon hurried toward them, but the ground was treacherous. He turned to see that his men were following him. Pahoran was beside him when a huge Lamanite parried at him with a staff. Gideon flailed his sword at him, cutting through the staff. Still the Lamanite came at him. Gideon admired the raw courage of the man.

There was a stinging pain at his back. He whirled around. Laman, the Lamanite king, his eyes dilated, pulled back from his sword lunge. Laman's eyes, stared at him with a look of pure hatred. "I will kill you," sounded harshly through his teeth.

The noise of the fight—metal clashing on wood and metal and the soft thud as sword met yielding body, the screams of the wounded and the sobs of the dying—all faded from Gideon's mind as he faced Laman. He didn't stop his momentum, but lunged forward. His blade met that of the Lamanite. He grimaced, changed hands with his sword, switching from Laman's left to his right, under his guard. He stamped his right foot forward, ignored Laman's sword, and caught him in the side. Laman tried to back away, slipped in the mud, and fell heavily. Gideon felt his sword's iron blade scrape against the king's ribs.

He suddenly felt very tired. His men swept past him, their swords out in front. He watched as they drove the enemy back. The Lamanites were now running. He heard a conch shell sounding loud above the battle. The Lamanite retreat turned into a rout as they ran towards the sound.

The fight was over. His warriors, still with the lust of battle in their eyes, filtered back to where he was standing. With them they brought several dozen prisoners. Gideon was surprised that so few of his men had been killed. Most stood there now, grinning at him. He grinned back, then picked up a broad leaf and wiped his sword blade.

* * *

"But Laman lived." Alma said, a question in his voice. "He is the one who, with his army, made us his prisoners in our city of Helam."

"Yes," Limhi said. "He was only wounded. Gideon and his men patched up Laman's wounds and brought him before me."

* * *

"We have captured King Laman," Gideon said gruffly. "He will not fight any more battles against us, nor direct his men to continue to rob us. We wanted you to see him before we slit his throat."

"No," replied Limhi. "We will not slay him. Bring the king in. I want to question him."

Gideon saluted and turned on his heel, returning in a few moments with the muddy and bloody Lamanite. Laman cast his eyes about him, looking vengefully at Gideon.

Limhi looked down at Laman. "Why have you broken the oath which you made with us."

"You ask me why I break the oath?" Laman exploded. "Your people have carried away our beautiful daughters. Their mothers and fathers are grieving. *You* broke the oath!" he shouted angrily.

"What?" Limhi asked, surprised. "Your daughters taken? When did this happen? I will immediately have a search made."

He looked at Gideon as if to find agreement, and added, "When we find the guilty ones they will be immediately brought to trial."

"Wait, sir," Gideon said. He walked forward and knelt for a moment before Limhi. Then he stood close to the throne where he could whisper to the young king. "Searching the people would be like turning wolves into your sheep herd. I promise you that none of our people would do such a thing. But I have a feeling who did it."

"Tell me," Limhi whispered in return.

"Your father's philandering priests!"

Limhi nodded. "That could well be."

Laman looked on, not hearing or understanding what they were saying.

"We searched all over for those priests so we could give them the death they deserved," Gideon said. "We never found them but we know they have been around because of things they've stolen."

Limni nodded again, waiting to see what else Gideon had to say.

"It seems simple," Gideon said. "The priests are hanging out in the wilderness. They needed female companionship so they kidnapped the daughters of the Lamanites."

"Yes," agreed Limhi. "That seems logical."

A youthful warrior came into the room, went straight to Gideon, and whispered to him.

Gideon frowned. "Your highness," he said, "we'd better tell Laman what happened. Our scouts have sighted the Lamanite army coming against us again. We caught them by surprise the first time, but if they come to battle again . . . " He shrugged, leaving the sentence unfinished.

Gideon looked at the Lamanite king who drooped wearily in the middle of the room. Then he turned back to Limhi. "My king, I don't think we have any choice. We need to pacify Laman so that he will pull back his army. At this time, my king, we can either be live slaves or dead heroes. Personally I prefer to stay living."

King Limhi nodded in agreement. He turned to King Laman and told him all that Gideon had said concerning the wicked priests.

King Laman was still angry, but he nodded. "I understand," he said. "Leave your swords and other weapons here and we will go forth to meet my warriors. I swear unto you with an oath that my people will not slay your people."

The three of them, the wounded King Laman in the lead, left the palace and walked out of the city. Behind them marched the unarmed Nephite army. Several times Gideon had to step forward to help King Laman. The Lamanite king was weak from his wound and the subsequent loss of blood, but he walked proudly, shaking off Gideon's assistance.

The Lamanite army, swords in hand, met them a half-hour's march from the city. Laman motioned for Limhi and Gideon to remain behind, then he went forward and prostrated himself before his own army. Gideon couldn't hear what he said, but apparently he commanded the Lamanites not to come to battle.

He was successful. He turned and waved at Limhi and Gideon, then two of his men formed a carriage with their arms, hoisted him up, turned, and began their march back to the Land of Shiblon.

* * *

"So you won your battle against the Lamanites." Alma said with a smile.

"Yes, but it was not the last one," sighed Limhi. "It wasn't but a few days until the Lamanites came into our land and began harrassing us. They didn't kill anyone, because of the oath that Laman made with us, but they slapped our peoples' faces, put heavy burdens on their backs, forced them to do menial tasks for them." He shrugged. "It was a hard time for my people."

"What happened then?"

"Something that shouldn't have happened. Over the years people became so upset that they continued to petition to me that we go to battle against the Lamanites." Limhi sighed again. "Finally, I yielded to their demands.

"Against Gideon's advice we gathered our people and went to battle." He shook his head sadly as he remembered. "It was a tragedy. We were so outnumbered and outfought that we lost almost half our warriors." He slowly exhaled through his nostrils. "There was much mourning throughout the Land of Nephi."

He paused as he remembered the awful scene of bloodshed after the battle. Alma waited.

"That is not the worst part. In our foolishness, we went back to battle a second time, and even a third. Each time we suffered the loss of many men. We finally admitted defeat. There was no way we could beat the Lamanites."

"What did you do?"

"What could we do? We submitted. We carried their heavy burdens. We listened humbly to their sarcasm. We accepted their beatings. Whatever the Lamanites wanted to do to us, we accepted."

A smile played at the edges of Limhi's mouth. "But some great good came out of it."

"How so?"

"For the first time, our people turned to God. They cried to Him to relieve them of their suffering and afflictions." Limhi's eyes misted. "For a long time there was no response, but at last our prayers were answered. Our crops started to produce more abundantly, the Lamanites became more compassionate towards us, and then, as a further answer to our prayers, a Nephite expedition found us and helped us to escape back to Zarahemla."

"That is a wonderful story."

Limhi nodded. "Yes, and I want you to meet Gideon and Ammon. They have been the two greatest instruments the Lord has used to give us our freedom once again."

"Who is Ammon?"

Limhi told Alma the story of how Ammon and the other fifteen men in his party had found them in the Land of Nephi, and had helped them to escape.

"Well, tell me the rest of the story. How did you make your escape?"

Smiling, Limhi answered. "It was Gideon again. I don't know what we would have done without him."

"You mean you had another battle?"

"No," Limhi smiled wryly. "The Lamanites were so numerous, there was no way we could beat them in a battle. We used more subtle means."

Alma listened as Limhi talked of Gideon.

"Gideon is a large man, and older and wiser than I. Sometimes he intimidated me," Limhi reflected. "Yet, he was always loyal and never became overbearing."

* * *

Gideon stood before the king once again. Ammon and his friends sat on one side of the throne room. Gideon cast his eyes upon the ground, not looking up until Limhi bid him.

"What is it, Gideon?"

"You've listened to me before, O king. Now I have a plan for us to escape the Lamanites. If it works we will slip past them slick as an eel."

"Well, speak up."

"On the north wall of the city is the gate where herds of sheep are usually driven."

"Isn't it heavily guarded by the Lamanites?" Ammon asked.

Gideon continued as if he hadn't heard Ammon's question. "It's a broad enough gate that many people or animals can pass through it at once. I have been watching the gate for the past few weeks. Every night the guards are as drunk as your father's priests on a feast night."

"Hmmm."

"If you were to send a proclamation among all of the people to gather their flocks and herds, and be ready to depart into the wilderness, I believe we could get all of the people out of the city while it's dark. Then it would just be a matter of staying ahead of the Lamanites in the wilderness."

"Gideon, it sounds like a good idea, but how do we know the guards will be drunk enough not to spread the alarm and stop us?"

Smiling, Gideon replied, "If you were to order me to do so, I could take extra wine rations to the guards. If it's strong enough, the Lamanites will sleep like babies while we leave the city. By the time they wake up from their drunken stupor we will be long gone."

Limhi smiled wryly. "Perhaps my father's vineyards will finally yield a positive result."

He asked, "When is the best time for us to leave?"

"The time of no moon is coming next week," Ammon said.

Gideon nodded. "If you were to send a proclamation tomorrow, there would be enough time to notify all of the people so they could be ready by that time."

"It is done. I shall call for my scribes immediately."

"Is there any danger of the Lamanites reading the proclamation?" Ammon asked.

"No. None of these lawless Lamanites know how to read," Gideon replied with a smile.

* * *

Limhi ended the story. "It went just as Gideon had predicted. That afternoon I sent out my messengers with the proclamation. They went to every house until all of the people were notified. At the time of no moon we slipped out of the city after dark. We took our gold and silver, our flocks and herds and went into the wilderness. Ammon and his men were excellent guides, and within a few weeks we arrived here in Zarahemla."

Alma nodded heartily. "The Lord truly blessed you and your people."

"That's true," Limhi said. "Now tell me the story of your escape."

Alma settled back in his chair, telling the story of his escape from the land of Nephi, the Waters of Mormon, and finally, the land of Helam.

Chapter 10

Establishing the Church

Warriors puffed and panted trying to keep up with Alma. Though his hair was thin and greying, Alma's tall body was firm and youthful. He still walked with the springy step which Esther so much admired. He looked back at the warriors, waved, and continued walking. The road was muddy underfoot, but his mouth was dry. He rolled some spittle around and swallowed. There was a small stream ahead just a few miles. He could wait until then for a drink.

He had traveled this road many times before. Each time he admired the skill and labors of King Mosiah's people. The road ran straight through the forest providing good accessibility between cities.

"What a task it would be," he had told Esther, "to do the traveling I do if I had to find my way through deep forest each time."

As he walked many thoughts filled his mind. Memories of his life in the lands of Nephi and Helam—lands he had loved even more than Zarahemla. Mountain climate in those lands was always moderate. Here it was always hot and humid. He looked around. Unchanging forest is all there is to see. He looked up with the thought. Tall moss-covered sapodilla trees formed an arch high above his head, and they dripped continuously! Even when the sky was blue and it wasn't raining, the trees continued raining on the ground below.

For the third time on this day, he unrolled the scroll he carried. Without missing a step, he read the passage he was memorizing. For years he had traveled between cities in the Land of Zarahemla. During that time he had memorized over two hundred sacred passages.

As he looked back on his experience in Zarahemla, Alma smiled. He had preached in every village and town in the land, walking to every one of them. His people—those who had lived in the Land of Helam and those who came from the Land of Nephi with King Limhi—were scattered to all of the cities and villages. King Mosiah had said that he felt their strength was needed in each community. Alma grinned as he thought, One reason I enjoy my travel so much between the cities is because I have a chance to see friends and family. He smiled as he thought of his daughter, Leesa, in Melek.

His thoughts were interrupted by a warrior's shout.

"Stop, Alma!"

He stopped and looked around curiously.

Warriors, awkward in their armor, ran to catch up to him. Tolo, in front, raised his spear high.

"What is it?" Alma asked.

Several warriors cried out together, "Jaguar!" "Big cat!"

He froze. Even the word caused a chill of fear to pass through him. He remembered how his son, Alma, had been maimed by one of the large cats. He looked where the warriors pointed. Above him, poised on a horizontal branch were two jaguars. Their mottled coats mimicked the play of sunlight and leaf shadows, and at first were almost invisible to Alma. One was lying on the branch, watching him with its yellow eyes. The second cat stood above, its tail outstretched and waving, its large head lowered as it watched the warriors approaching. Another chill went through Alma. The Lord had promised that nothing would harm him until his work was done, but still . . . ! He had heard numerous tales of how these huge cats dropped on unsuspecting travelers, breaking their necks with one swipe of massive legs.

As yelling warriors approached, both cats stood, their large black spots contrasting with their tawny-brown coats. They stretched languidly on the branch, appearing unconcerned with those below, then together the cats loped across the branches into the forest.

Alma thanked Tolo and the others for being so alert, then as they dropped back again, he continued walking, alone with his thoughts. Though Mosiah had assigned the squad of warriors to accompany him, they provided no company for him. Soldiers carried their swords and spears. He was content to carry his scroll, pleased to have time as he walked to think about his life and to study the scriptures.

Forgetting the interruption, his thoughts returned to the time since their arrival in Zarahemla. As he analyzed it, 490 years had passed since Lehi and his family left Jerusalem. He had been born in the 426th year. That would mean he was now sixty-four years of age. He held one of his hands before his face. The skin was still tight, and although it was deeply tanned, he could not yet see any brown age spots. Really, he thought to himself, I don't mind getting old; except there is no one to whom I can confer responsibility for the Church. Zoram is out fighting Lamanites and apparently enjoying himself. Young Alma? He frowned. Why was his youngest son so irresponsible?

He mentally listed young Alma's attributes. At twenty-two he is well-schooled as a scribe. In fact, Alma thought, he can write Hebrew and Egyptian better than I. He is strong and healthy. And handsome! Alma smiled as he thought of how the girls in Zarahemla cast their eyes at his son. Maybe one of young Alma's problems was he was too handsome and too well-educated.

He glanced at the scroll again. The passage he was memorizing was Jacob's teaching concerning those who were puffed up with knowledge. "When they are learned they think they are wise, and they hearken not unto the counsel of God, for they set it aside, supposing they know of themselves, wherefore their wisdom is foolishness and it profiteth them not. And they shall perish."

He re-rolled the scroll. His lips moved as he repeated the scripture. Yes, young Alma's problem was one of supposing he knew of himself. He failed to hearken unto the counsel of God. Alma sighed.

Ah, there was the stream. He stepped to the side of the road and set his scroll carefully against a tree. Removing his tunic, he lay alongside the stream and drank deeply. Oh, fresh water did taste good. He cupped some water in his hands and poured it over his head. The warriors caught up with him and were soon lying by the stream, quenching their thirst.

The sun's warmth and the long hike made Alma sleepy. He dozed, his back against the tree. The murmuring of the clear stream beside him soothed his mind. Eyes closed, he drifted between sleep and wakefulness. His mind went back to his most choice experience since arriving in Zarahemla. Alma drowsily smiled at the memory. What an occasion!

* * *

A mighty roar went up from the people as Alma finished his first sermon in Zarahemla. The accolade was almost embarrassing to him. He walked down the steps, seeking out Esther with his eyes. People milled about, patting him on the back, smiling, congratulating him.

Limhi stopped him. "Alma, I felt the Lord's spirit burning within me when you spoke—especially during that part about the Lord leading us out of bondage."

"That is wonderful," Alma said.

Limhi took Alma's hands. "Alma, we have a desire to be baptized. You are the one who knows what to do. Some of your people have told me of the great feelings they experienced after baptism. What must we do to be baptized?"

"Baptism is open to all," Alma said quietly. "The requirements are simple: have faith in Jesus Christ who will come, and repent of any transgressions."

"I have met both of those requirements."

"Then there is nothing preventing you from being baptized."

"What of my people? Baptism is their wish, also."

Alma put his arm around Limhi's shoulders, walking with him towards where Esther was waiting. The king's request brought gladness to him.

"We will set a time when everyone who desires baptism may be baptized. But first, I must get permission from King Mosiah."

"I will tell my people!" Limhi said as he hurried away.

Esther waited with eyes aglow. Alma put his arm around her and guided her back towards their temporary home. No words were spoken for some time. As they neared their tent, Alma sighed contentedly.

"What is it?"

He squeezed her waist. "Limhi has requested that he and all his people be baptized."

"But there are several thousand people!"

"I know."

"But how ? . . ."

He put his finger on her lips, silencing her question. "As soon as I have received permission from King Mosiah, I will ask the other priests whom I have ordained to help. There are more than twenty priests. With their help we can accomplish this beautiful task without problems."

While Esther prepared their evening meal, Alma hurried back to the palace. He gained an audience with King Mosiah and presented his request.

Mosiah stepped forward and placed his hands on Alma's arms. "My friend," he said. "I appreciate your consideration in asking me. My father, Benjamin, and grandfather, Mosiah, were leaders of both the civil government and the church. That is a greater responsibility than I want. Therefore, from this time forward, we will divide responsibilities. I will be civil ruler and you will handle all church responsibilities.

"You indicated the Lord designated you as High Priest. Continue in that role. As high priest perform all religious functions: organize churches, ordain priests and teachers, baptize and perform any other tasks which relate to the spiritual life of this people."

Alma bowed low. "Be it as you desire, my king."

He hurried home to tell Esther.

"Oh, Alma, that is wonderful," she said.

"Yes, dear, the Lord has directed me rightly." He hugged her. "Here in Zarahemla we will have a similar organization to what we established in Helam."

He wrote a proclamation, and the following day sent it by messengers to all who were still gathered in Zarahemla. The proclamation announced that a baptismal service would held at the big bend of the River Sidon at dawn the following day, and that all those who wanted to be baptized should be there.

He called a meeting of those he had set apart as priests of the Church. As they filed into the meeting hall, he looked with pleasure on Helam, Amalakiahah, Balzar, Nephihah, Zephany, Amarta and the others.

"Brethren," he said. "Ours is a great responsibility. On the morrow, several thousand of our brothers and sisters will be gathered at the river wanting to be baptized. Baptizing so many people is too large a task for me to accomplish by myself. Your help and your priesthood is needed. All of you have performed baptisms while we dwelt in Helam. Prepare yourselves today with fasting and prayer. Remember the Lord's house is a house of order. There should be no confusion in people's minds as to the purpose or the form of baptism."

He demonstrated once more the proper form, using the words which the Lord taught him.

His final instructions were, "Each of you bring with you a scribe to record names of those whom you baptize." He paused and closed his eyes as another thought came into his mind. He nodded to himself.

Opening his eyes, he again spoke to his priests. "When we have finished baptizing we will go with these people to their various cities. There we will organize churches so everyone can worship the true God."

Alma was so excited he couldn't sleep. He rolled and tossed on his mat until finally, just to avoid disturbing Esther further, he arose, lighted a candle, and in a corner of the tent studied scriptures. He looked often and sadly at the mat where his son, young Alma, slept. His son had come home late with the smell of wine on his breath.

Alma interspersed his readings with prayer: prayer for the Lord's spirit to be with them on the morrow, and prayer that young Alma would repent and turn to the Lord.

Dawn found him and his priests already at the river. He selected a wide spot where the bank sloped gently into the water. Here there was no current as water eddied around the broad bend, forming pools of still, quiet water.

By noon the baptizing was finished. Alma wearily walked forth from the river. Thousands of those baptized lined the river banks. They seemed reluctant to leave what had become for them a holy place. Looks of joy on their faces indicated an outpouring of the spirit.

Alma called his scribe, Aaron, to him. As Aaron walked towards him, disappointment filled Alma's heart. Young Alma should have been the one standing before him as scribe. He had awakened his son early and asked him to attend the baptism as his scribe, but young Alma had refused.

He recalled his own words. "It is important, Alma, to record names of those baptized. This will become part of our record."

Young Alma sullenly asked, "Why do we need records?"

"We must carry on the traditions begun by Nephi. All that happens in the Church—baptisms, the sermons of leaders and priests, the history of the people—all needs to be recorded."

"Why?"

"The Lord is using our experience to teach generations of people who will live on this land at some future time. This land will be a promised land to them if they will learn from our experience and will serve the Lord and each other. If they don't, they will be destroyed."

Young Alma sneered and then made some excuse as to why he couldn't be at the baptism.

Now Alma put his hand on his scribe's shoulder. "How many baptisms, Aaron."

Aaron counted the names on the bark paper. "Two hundred thirty-nine."

Alma looked at other priests coming dripping from the water and mused aloud, "Twenty-two priests. If each baptized two-hundred—that would be over four thousand baptisms today!"

Two things marred an otherwise perfect day. First was the hurt of young Alma's refusal to attend. The other was the void caused by Esther's absence from the baptism. Esther was ill with fever. In fact, Alma recalled, Esther has been ill much of the time since coming to Zarahemla. There had been little sickness in the mountains of Helam. Here someone was always sick with fever.

* * *

Alma sat up and then leaned over for another drink from the stream. He reached in his pouch and brought out dried fruit and nuts Esther had put in for his lunch. As he munched, he thought of all that had been accomplished since that day of baptism. His priests had established new churches in every city: Zarahemla, Gideon, Manti, Melek, Sidom, Ammonihah, and Judea.

What makes the Church strong, he thought, is the unity of the churches. Though there are seven churches and many branches of the Church, there is only one Church. Priests and teachers only teach those things which I teach. Everything I teach comes from the scriptures or from words which the Lord has planted in my mind. Now the Church is known as the Church of God and the people are known as the people of God. Never in my life, Alma thought, has the outpouring of the Lord's Spirit been so strong among a people. We are truly blessed and have prospered in the land.

He knelt by the stream, took one last long drink, and rose to resume his journey. Putting on his tunic, he bent over, picked up the scroll, and was again on his way. The squad of warriors followed close behind.

Today his destination was the city of Gideon. He smiled in anticipation of being there. The city was named after crusty Gideon who led Limhi's people in battle against the Lamanites. He had become Alma's good friend and they had spent many hours sipping sweet, hot chocolate and sharing stories.

Alma glanced at the sun; two more hours. Once more he unrolled the scroll and read the passage he was memorizing. "The cunning plan of the evil one . . . the vainness and frailties and foolishness of man."

As his long paces covered miles along the still muddy road, Alma pondered that scripture. How much learning should people have? At what point in their learning did they "think they were wise and hearken not unto the counsel of God"?

Again Alma's thoughts turned to Alma, his son. Alma was learned. He had been taught in writing and in the scriptures. He learned astronomy from temple priests. But he was not using his knowledge to serve the Lord. Perhaps that was the key: knowledge was not as important as the *use of knowledge*. He nodded his head in understanding, Yes. Knowledge by itself was virtually worthless. Only use of knowledge counted. Is that what the Lord meant when he said, "To be learned is good if they hearken unto the counsels of God"?

As he walked towards the city of Gideon, Alma recalled how King Mosiah had invited him, soon after his arrival in Zarahemla, to the library room in the palace where all the records were kept. He pictured the room in his mind. Again he felt the wonderment as he knelt by stacks of gold plates; his feeling of joy as he reverently held the Small Plates of Nephi and slowly turned the fine, gold pages. He stood in awe before the special inlaid box holding the brass plates. What a history they contained. To think the first one to write upon them was Joseph after he had been sold into slavery in Egypt. Now the plates were here before him. The experience was almost more than he could comprehend.

Against another wall were rolls and rolls of parchment and bark paper. Mosiah smiled in understanding as Alma picked up one after another, reverently unrolling each and reading from them. Here were contained sermons of King Mosiah and King Benjamin. Alma had heard of King Benjamin's final sermon and now here it was in his hands! He made a vow. As soon as time permitted he would return to this room and read from Benjamin's writings.

Alma gasped with pleasure as Mosiah showed him the collected memorabilia of the Nephites: the sword of Laban, wrapped and oiled, the Liahona, a compass which guided Lehi to the promised land; and the interpreters and the twenty-four gold plates which were found with the remains of the Jaredite civilization. The shelves and cupboards were all filled with treasures of history. He didn't dare touch any, but stood in awe before them.

As excited as he was about the collected objects, it was the records and writings which thrilled him most. He turned to Mosiah and pointed to the scrolls.

"The words of your father, Benjamin. Have they been given to the people?"

"When father gave his closing sermon," Mosiah responded, "copies were made and given to the people."

"How long has that been?"

Mosiah shrugged, "Seven years."

"My people and the people of King Limhi did not hear your father's sermon. Could copies be made for us?"

"Of course."

"And Mosiah . . . "

"Yes."

"May I assign scribes to inscribe your father's writings onto plates of gold so they will endure with the plates of Nephi?"

"Good idea. And while your scribes are here, they should also inscribe your writings and the records of Limhi's people on gold plates. That will make our records complete."

As Alma neared the city of Gideon, he thought proudly of how his scribes had worked almost continuously since that time copying records; inscribing them on gold plates and thus preserving them for future generations.

The library of Mosiah was a treasure house of learning and Alma drew often from those treasures. While in Zarahemla he spent much of his time in the library, reading firsthand the writings of Lehi, Nephi and Jacob. He reverently handled the precious brass plates, reading the words of Joseph, Moses, Isaiah and the other prophets. As scribes finished copies of scrolls, he carefully stored them in his own library.

King Benjamin's last sermon was masterful. He had read the words many times, savoring the meanings. What greatness King Benjamin displayed through his words—words which rang with sincerity, humility and power. Many of the scriptures he had memorized had come from King Benjamin's writings: words prophesying the Savior who was to come, words of wisdom and counsel.

Alma especially enjoyed King Benjamin's counsel concerning service: that "when you are in the service of your fellow beings, you are only in the service of your God." He longed to publish that scripture to all his people, for there were still some who advocated priestcraft, feeling that priests should be paid for service rendered.

He mused aloud, "Service is what Godhood is all about."

Contained in the records was the covenant which King Benjamin had his people sign following his last address. It read: "We enter into a covenant with our God to do His will, and to be obedient to His commandments in all things that He shall command us, all the remainder of our days, that we may not bring upon ourselves a never-ending torment, as has been spoken by the angel, that we may not drink out of the cup of the wrath of God."

In the scrolls, Alma read the names of those who signed statements of commitment at the end of Benjamin's address. I wonder how many of them are still committed? he asked himself. People make covenants in all sincerity, then when the first tough trial comes along, many backslide. Yet, without trial there is really no test of a person's commitment.

Alma's thoughts then focused on what had been accomplished with the sacred records since his arrival in Zarahemla. A host of scribes had copied records onto gold plates. All Benjamin's writings and part of his own and Limhi's records had been permanently inscribed. That accomplishment gave him great satisfaction. There was only one more task for the scribes: The twenty-four gold plates found by Limhi's scouts and brought to Mosiah had not been translated.

I need to meet with Mosiah and help him translate the plates and we can then inscribe them for posterity, he thought. Then the records will be current.

As the temples and buildings of Gideon came into sight through the jungle, he sighed once again. With the joy of the baptism, the establishment of the Church throughout the land of Zarahemla, and all the pleasure of having the records made permanent, he was still sorrowful. Two things still caused him great agony—the illness of his beloved Esther, and the lack of righteousness of his son, Alma.

Chapter 11

Wayward Son

Gaunt, tall, and looking youthful in spite of his age, the warrior stood before Alma.

Shifting his weight nervously from foot to foot, Gideon said, "I don't like to be a tale-bearer, but there is something you should know."

Alma looked at this man who had become his friend. Though he felt Gideon's seriousness, he still smiled inwardly. From the very first, Alma had been impressed with the straightforwardness and lack of subtlety in the man. Now, Gideon was about to unburden himself.

Alma sat on the proffered stool and motioned for Gideon to speak.

There was a slight hesitancy in Gideon, then he spoke. "Alma, it's your soothsaying son I'm concerned about."

"Zoram?" Alma felt his stomach tighten with anxiety.

"No, your younger son, Alma."

Alma leaned forward, attentively.

"For years you've been making your rounds of various cities and villages, establishing the Lord's church, instructing priests, and preaching to the people."

Alma nodded, impatient to hear what Gideon was getting at.

"But your preaching's as worthless as a wooden sword when others follow right behind you cutting down the very doctrines and principles you have taught," Gideon said stoutly.

"And who does that?"

"Darn it, that's what I'm trying to tell you. It's your son—and those toady tagtails who follow him."

Alma leaned back slowly, a gnawing feeling rising into his chest. "Alma?"

"Yes, he and those silky sons of King Mosiah preach their pernicious rebellious religion in every village and city."

"What do they preach?"

Gideon rose, walked to the window, then turned to face Alma. "They teach that it's stupid to worship a god that can't be felt and seen and touched. They bring with them a stone idol—the head of a sensual serpent. They call their god, Zimpoc."

Alma felt so weary. He shook his head. "Idol worship amongst our people?" He paused, attempting to digest what Gideon was telling him. "How do people react?"

Shrugging, the gray-haired warrior replied. "Most of the older people are hanging onto the truth like a tick in a dog's ear."

"Then who follows those who preach against the word of Christ?"

"Long-haired young rebels who were children at the time King Benjamin spoke to the people; rebels who either didn't listen or else didn't understand his words."

"But they have been taught by their priests and parents."

"That's true, Alma, but they believe that the traditions of their fathers are hogwash. Worshipping something tangible like sun or a stone idol is easier for them. There are apparently some people who would rather worship something they actually see. The God you and I teach of requires more faith." He shrugged his shoulders. "So, many of our people have dropped out of the church and are following your son."

It was beyond Alma's understanding how anyone could depart from the teachings of the Savior—especially his own son. He asked wearily, "How many people have we lost?"

Again, Gideon shrugged. "Hard to say. There are people who like the rugged vitality of Alma and his friend, Nehor. Alma flatters them with words. They like what he says. Your son," he said admiringly, "is smart. He is a darn good leader and is building up a huge following."

"What else do they teach?"

"They don't seem to teach anything positive. They spend their time teaching what *not* to believe."

"Such as?"

"They teach that the resurrection of the dead is just a fairytale."

"And?"

"They don't believe in the coming of Christ, or in baptism, or . . . "

Alma didn't hear the rest of what Gideon was saying. He was sick inside. His son was teaching people not to believe in Jesus Christ, when all of his life that belief had been the primary teaching in their home. Words of King Benjamin came again to him:

"Wo, wo unto him who knoweth that he rebelleth against God! For salvation cometh to none such except it be through repentance and faith on the Lord Jesus Christ."

Gideon had finished talking and was looking with concern at him. Alma swallowed hard, a resolve forming within him. He stood and placed his hands on Gideon's shoulders.

"My friend, I appreciate your willingness to tell me what is happening. I don't know what to do yet, but we must stop this movement before it infects the church with its pernicious doctrines."

Gideon squeezed his arm as he said, "There's more."

"Go ahead. Let's hear it all."

"Things are starting to get rough for those who don't accept their teachings."

"What do you mean?"

"Unbelievers stop our people on their way to worship and beat them. Several faithful ones have come to me for my word and protection." He spread his hands helplessly before Alma.

Alma sat down once more, holding his head in his hands. Why hadn't he done something earlier? He had suspected young Alma had rebelled against the church, yet he had refused to accept his own thinking. Having a son reared in the gospel, with knowledge of Jesus Christ—and turning against that knowledge was more than he could understand.

He stood, resolute in what he must do. "I'm afraid my age is catching up with me, my friend. I must rest now."

Gideon helped him to the bedroom.

Alma did not rest. He alternated between worrying about Esther's illness and the waywardness of his son. A memory haunted him: he saw himself years ago at the breakfast table with Young Alma.

* * *

At breakfast, he watched as Young Alma listlessly stirred his corn-meal porridge. His son glanced across the table at him, then quickly looked back into his bowl, closed his eyes, and pushed the bowl from him. He looked up when his father asked, "Son, I can tell your mind is troubled. Please tell me what it is. Perhaps I can help."

Uncontrolled tears rolled down young Alma's face. Alma listened as his son seemed to pour out his heart. "Father, I used to think that I really wanted to be like you. Now, I don't feel I can be like you. You are a person people love and enjoy being around. A person they look up to with respect."

He paused a moment. Alma reached over and gently brushed the tears from his son's cheeks. He was aware his own eyes were brimming.

"You know," his son continued. "I don't really care whether I am rich or famous. I just want people to know I'm alive—that I can be a leader. I want people to treat me like they treat you—with respect."

Alma asked, "Didn't your classmates respect you in the school of the scribes?"

"Yes, but . . . "

"And don't your fellow warriors respect you now in your warrior training?"

"Yes, but . . . "

"Do you feel that your mother and I respect you?"

"Yes."

"It seems to me you are getting all the respect one young man can handle."

"Father, that isn't the kind of respect I mean." He ducked his head above his bowl of cereal.

As he sat across from his son, Alma could feel the deep yearning in his son's heart. He hadn't thought about it before, but now he realized that, in young Alma's thinking, becoming like his father was impossible for him to achieve. As long as he was in the position he was, perhaps there would never be an opportunity for the youthful Alma to do the same thing. He thought of the scriptures he had read, how Laman and Lemuel rebelled against their father. Could it have been a similar thing? Could they have rebelled because they saw no possibility for themselves to become prophets like their father, Lehi?

But no, there was Nephi. Nephi had respected his father but he also wanted to be like him. Nephi had done the right things to accomplish just that purpose. Each child seemed to be so different.

Young Alma scraped his chair back on the dirt floor and hurriedly left the table. As he ducked out the door Alma hurried to his feet.

* * *

Alma lay on his couch in Gideon's house thinking of that scene with his son. That incident had occurred several years ago and it was the last conversation of any import Alma had with his son. Could he have seen then what was happening? Should his son's words have given him insight into future problems?

After a sleepless night in Gideon, he departed the next day for Sidom. Punctuated by his nagging questions at every step, the road seemed longer than it ever had before. Where had he gone wrong? What had happened to Young Alma? Why had he turned against the Church and his father's teachings? These and many more questions plagued him as he walked.

He had been a good counselor to the many people in the church. Why was it he could not be effective with his own son? Zoram and Netta and Leesa had all listened to him and turned out all right. They married well in the Church. He did enjoy them and their children. But young Alma? His youngest son had never married. Why? Alma shook his head at the next thought he had. Perhaps young Alma didn't need marriage. Could he have taken up with concubines?

He thought back over the years since they escaped from Lamanites in Helam and made their way to Zarahemla. He had devoted almost his entire time and energy to building up the Church in the Land of Zarahemla, only to see it now being torn down—and by his own son! That was more than he could bear.

Another recurring thought surfaced. Who is to take my place? I am almost seventy years of age. Most of the priests I ordained are as old as I. "Oh, Alma," he cried softly to himself so the accompanying warriors wouldn't hear him. "Come back to me. Be my son once again and prepare yourself to be God's servant." Tears ran unheeded down his cheeks.

* * *

Conditions of rebellion were even worse in Sidom. When Alma arrived there the city was in an uproar. He made his way to the home of Nephihah, the priest over the church. Nephihah led him to the roof. From their vantage point they saw thousands of people in the streets, swaying, shaking and shouting to heavy drumbeats.

Alma shouted to be heard above the din. "What is happening?"

"A new religion—worship of a serpent-god, Zimpoc."

Closing his eyes and shaking his head, Alma sunk to the parapet and moaned audibly. "O Alma, my son. You do not know the evil you have done." He looked up at Nephihah. "Our church members?"

"More than a third gone." Nephihah made a wry face. "Many of the rest now fear for their lives. The city has gone wild, and persecution is all directed at the Church of God."

"This must be stopped," Alma said. Then he added silently to himself, Even if it means the life of my son.

After doing what he could to hold the people together in Sidom, he visited the churches in Melek, Judea, Cumeni, and Manti. The story was the same: Those who opposed the Church of God were highly organized and had disrupted every city. Sorrowfully Alma made his way back to Zarahemla.

He was so relieved to see Esther. She had been a source of strength to him from the beginning. She looked better. Perhaps the fever had left her. He held her close, squeezing her until she finally gasped.

"Alma, what is the matter?"

He looked at her with tear-reddened eyes. "It is Alma," he said, shaking his head sorrowfully.

"Alma? Has something happened to our son?" Her voice rose, filled with concern.

"Nothing physical has harmed him, my dear. But what has happened to him is much worse."

"Worse?" Alma sensed the worry in her voice.

He told her of his travels, of what Gideon and the other priests had told him. He looked at her sorrowfully. "My love, I am getting old. I will not

be able to make many more journeys. What will happen to the Church—
to all we have tried to do over the years?"

* * *

Esther, though still weak from her bout with the fever, cradled Alma's
head in her hands, stroking his temples gently with her fingers. She had
lived with this man for over forty years but never had she seen him so
despondent. His world seemed to be crumbling around him. He acted as
if he no longer even wanted to live.

"What will you do?" she asked.

"I don't know. I just don't know."

She pushed him away so she could look into his eyes. "Remember when
the Lamanites became so oppressive to us in Helam?"

He nodded.

"What did you do then?"

"Oh, Esther. I know what you are suggesting, but I have been praying
continuously for years. And the problem is worse now."

She was desperate to break his mood. Perhaps shock treatment would
do. "Don't you trust the Lord?" She felt his body stiffen against her.

He looked at her fiercely. "Of course I trust the Lord." Unconsciously,
his voice had risen in volume.

"You are always preaching to other people to trust in the Lord and he
will take care of your righteous desires."

Alma sighed and drooped his head. "That is true, my love. Right now,
though, I am so overwhelmed by the consequences of what Alma is doing
that I cannot think of anything else."

"Consequences?"

"Yes. All the prophets have spoken forcefully about those who know
truth and rebel against it." He paused. "For instance, Jacob taught, 'Wo
unto him that has the law given, that has all the commandments of God,
like unto us, and that transgresseth them, and that wasteth the days of
his probation, for awful is his state!'

"And Abinadi spoke strongly on the subject, saying, 'The Lord redeemeth
none that rebel against him and die in their sins. Those who have known
the commandments of God and have not kept them have no part in the
first resurrection.' " He buried his head in Esther's long grey tresses.

"Have you given up hope?" she asked quietly.

He held her at arm's length, looking deeply into her eyes. Then he sighed.
"No, I haven't given up hope. I still hope. I have taught that when a per-
son gives up hope he also discontinues his communication with God.
Thank goodness I can still hope; I can still communicate."

She said nothing, just held him. It still amazed her, after all her years with Alma, that grown men needed as much comforting as little children. As she held him, her own thoughts went to her son, Alma. What would happen to him? How could she and Alma turn him back to the paths of righteousness? Even though he had strayed, she had faith he would return.

With his head cradled to her, Alma asked, "Esther?"

"Yes, my love."

"Why do you think our son has departed from church and family?"

Esther had asked herself the same question many times. She answered, "I am not sure, Alma. Perhaps there are several reasons."

Alma pulled away from her, looking down into her eyes. "Is it because I have neglected him?"

She did not want to answer, but she responded, "That may be part of the problem, but I feel it goes even deeper."

"What do you mean?"

"I have a feeling he doesn't like himself. Deep inside he thinks he can't be any good."

"But why would he think that?"

"I don't know for sure. He was the baby of the family. He didn't share as many responsibilities as the other children."

"That shouldn't make him dislike himself."

"Not by itself. But I felt many times as he was growing up he was unsure of himself—surrounded by such strong people that he developed an attitude of inferiority."

"Why didn't you ever talk to me about those feelings?"

"Oh, Alma, you were always so busy. I didn't want to bother you with things which would probably work themselves out anyway."

"But they haven't."

Esther ducked her head. "Yes, I know."

"Are you saying that Alma didn't feel anyone liked him?"

"Yes, but it is deeper than that. Remember how he always worked so hard at trying to be everyone's friend. And how, usually, the friends he made were those who were the underdogs—those who had been kicked around, like his friend, Nehor."

"Yes, but what does that . . ."

She impatiently interrupted him. "Don't you see? He didn't feel he could make friends with those he thought were superior. He perceived himself differently."

Alma frowned and nodded. Esther could see he was struggling with this new train of thought. He mumbled. "I am still not sure what effect this has on his behavior now—his rebellion against church and family."

"I think Alma needs to feel accepted and wanted. He is trying to find his own place in life." Her eyes misted. "I think our son is a very unhappy person. He feels he cannot compete against you with those who are righteous, so he has set himself up in opposition to you."

"Then that is why whenever I would criticize him? . . . "

"Yes; the first word of criticism and then there seemed to be a devil inside him which took over."

* * *

As Alma busied himself strengthening the Zarahemla church, he pondered Esther's words. What wisdom she showed, he thought. Why couldn't I have seen the things which she saw? Why didn't I notice we were losing this choice son?

Alma visited each of the church leaders in Zarahemla. So far, here in the capital, order prevailed. Alma wondered how long it would be until even Zarahemla was affected by apostasy and persecution.

He was thankful for Esther's support and firmness. What would he do without her strength! He had known all along the only course open to him was continuing and fervent prayer. Now he must get on with it.

As he made his way into the forest, there began to be a sound of sighing in the air; wind was rising. Then rain came, gentle at first; just a little patter. The wind died and then the rain turned into a steady, fine drizzle almost like mist.

Alma, drenched and discouraged, arrived at his favorite glen. The unrelieved gloom of the glen did not help his attitude. The sky was dark, the forest darker still, and rain fell relentlessly in small drops. He dropped wearily to his knees and gazed at the surrounding forest. He knelt there, getting wetter and wetter.

"Father, where did I go wrong? What has happened to my son? What can I do?"

For hours he prayed, miserable though he was. His old, stiff body ached from being in a kneeling position for such a long time. Alma shut out the pain and continued with his prayer.

"Please, Father, I will do whatever is necessary to bring him back. Help me!"

As he prayed, great tears of grief rolled down his cheeks, mingling with the rain. The tears and rain were ignored, along with the aches he felt. His eyes squinted shut and he didn't even see the forest he loved. This was his own sacred glen, a place of respite and peace. Here the Lord had often spoken to him. Why not now? Why couldn't he get the same sweet quiet voice in his consciousness, or the warm peaceful feeling in his bosom? Now he prayed for peace once again.

Many times during past years his prayers had been the same. "What can I do to help Alma? How can I bring him back to the fold?"

He prayed on, "Father, ever since the time of Abinadi, I have served Thee totally. My whole life has been devoted to Thy service."

Then thoughts came to him. Even sometimes to the neglecting of my family. His mind wandered to scenes of the past, times when he was called away from home to administer to the sick, or pray with a family, or preach to a congregation. He thought of the support and uncomplaining attitude Esther had given throughout his ministry. Never had she attempted to stop him from doing what he thought was his duty.

Missed opportunities of association with young Alma passed through his mind. His son had been well taught. He was just fourteen when they had fled from the Lamanites and left the Land of Helam. Prior to that time he had been enrolled in the school of the scribes where he had learned to read and write the language of the people. He, himself, had taught his son about the Savior and the Plan of Salvation. As Alma reminisced about his relationship with his son, he realized the only thing he hadn't given his son was enough of his time. He reached up and grasped his hair in both hands, wrenching his head downward in self condemnation.

He cried aloud, "Oh, Father, that I could live that part of my life over. That I would give more time to the son whom I love so very much."

He moaned aloud in anguish of spirit.

Then there was stillness in the forest. The usual forest sounds— birds singing, insects buzzing, trees cracking and creaking—failed to penetrate his consciousness. Even the soft patter of the rain seemed to cease. Earth itself seemed to stand still.

The forest echoed with a voice—not the still voice which he had so often heard, but a voice of thunder filled the little glen with a cacophony of sound, reverbrating off trees and ground. Alma huddled where he was.

My son. Peace be unto thy soul. That which Alma is doing will soon end. He has been taught well in the Gospel. The time will come when he will return to the fold. He will serve me as you have served me. Have patience, my son.

As had happened so many times before, feelings of warmth and peace filled Alma's bosom. For the first time he realized that being slaves to the Lamanites in Helam had not been a trial of his faith. Young Alma's rebellion was a personal trial he had to suffer that he might receive the blessings. He sobbed with thanksgiving, "Praise Thee, O Lord. Praise Thy name forever!" For the first time in years, Alma was at peace with himself.

Chapter 12

Call to Repentance

REPORT ANY ATTEMPTS OF PEOPLE TO INTIMIDATE CHURCH MEMBERS. GET NAMES OF THOSE WHO PREACH DISSENSION OR WHO PERSECUTE THE MEMBERS OF THE CHURCH. REPORT ANY MEMBERS WHO ARE USING THIS DISRUPTION AS EXCUSE TO COMMIT SIN.

Alma read the proclamation again. He felt so frustrated. He laid his brush down and picked up the scroll he had received from Melek this morning.

"Our people are being threatened daily to forsake the teachings of the Church. Those who listen are being enticed by false prophets to ignore such sins as idolatry, adultery, and even murder."

From every city came similar messages. Alma read each message, convinced the time had come spoken of by Nephi: "In that day shall churches be built up which are not unto the Lord. They shall contend one with another and shall deny the Holy Ghost and power of God. They shall say unto the people: 'Behold there is no God today. He has done his work and has given his power unto men. Eat, drink, and be merry, for tomorrow we die; and it shall be well with us.' "

Alma thought of the next verse. "O those who are puffed up in the pride of their hearts, and all those who preach false doctrines, and all those who commit whoredoms, and pervert the right way of the Lord, wo, wo, wo be unto them, saith the Lord God Almighty, for they shall be thrust down to hell!"

Alma could read no further. The phrase "wo be unto them for they shall be thrust down to hell," rang repeatedly through his mind. He dropped on his knees from his chair.

"O Lord," he cried aloud. "Nephi did see our time. He did see what would happen to our people. Help us overcome this evil. Help my son to see truth and to repent of his evil ways before he seals his fate and is condemned to be thrust down to hell."

He picked up the scroll with his message to the priests of the several cities. In bold letters at the bottom he added with firm brush strokes, PLEASE READ NEPHI'S PREDICTION TO THE PEOPLE. He wrote the scripture reference, picked up the scroll and took it to a scribe in the next room.

When enough copies were made, Alma called for king's runners and soon the proclamation was on its way to every city. Alma felt better. At least he was doing something positive to counter the threat of idol worshippers and apostates.

After all runners were gone, Alma sat wearily back at his table. Motioning to his servant, Artubus, he prepared himself to see the young people with whom he had requested an audience. Five young men and two young women—Alma judged them not to be over twenty-five years of age—entered the room.

This was the fourth group he had interviewed this week. He leaned forward in his chair and looked at each of them. They were handsome men and charming women but something was lacking. They kept their eyes on the floor and wouldn't look at him, almost as if they lived in a different world. He sincerely wanted to find out their thoughts.

Alma stood and walked around his table to stand in front of them. "I understand you are not members of the Church of God," he stated.

One of the young men, obviously a leader, shook his head, mumbling something which Alma could not understand.

Alma walked up to stand before the young man. "What is your name?"

"Ekalon."

Alma waited a few moments, then asked, "Ekalon, is there something which our priests teach which you don't understand?"

Ekalon looked up, defiance in his eyes. "We do not believe in the foolish traditions of our fathers!"

"Foolish traditions?"

"Yes. Traditions that a god will come to earth and become a human; and traditions which say people will come alive again after they die."

"Are there other things you don't believe?"

One young women spoke up behind Ekalon. "We don't believe in all the stupid rules, either."

"Stupid rules?"

"Yes, stupid rules!" she shouted. "Rules that take away our freedom. 'Don't do this!' and 'don't do that!' " She looked defiantly at Alma. "We make our own rules."

Alma attempted to reason with them but to no avail; it was almost like butting his head against the proverbial stone wall. He finally gave up and dismissed them.

Artabus came back into the room. "Do you want to see any more rebellious ones?"

Alma shook his head. "No. I'm afraid it is no use. Their minds are made up. They won't listen to anything I say."

Artabus bowed and quietly left the room, leaving Alma with his thoughts. He walked back to his table, picked up his brush, and opened the journal in which he had been writing. With quick brush strokes he wrote,

"Because of their unbelief many people cannot understand the word of God. Their hearts are hardened, and they will not be baptized or join the church."

The next week was quiet. Alma devoted himself to Esther and to his writing. Even in quiet periods there never seemed enough time to get everything accomplished. He greatly enjoyed evening walks through the city with Esther, and visits of his children and grandchildren. His family had certainly grown. He missed Zoram, who was still fighting Lamanites on the borders of the land, but his heart swelled with pride as he saw how his grandsons and granddaughters were growing.

If only I can soon resolve the problem of my son, Alma, he thought, my life will be so happy. I have so much for which to be thankful.

His peace was short-lived. On the Sabbath, Gideon and a delegation from his city arrived with four accused sinners. Alma interviewed each, and listened to Gideon's and others' testimony who came to witness against the offenders. Before Alma decided what to do with them, Joshua arrived with six prisoners from Melek. By noon of the first day of the week, there were twenty-two defendants standing before Alma along with their accusers. Each had been interviewed and had refused to repent. Now Alma was not sure what to do. He had not expected such a quick response to his proclamation. What was he going to do with these people?

An idea came to him. Let Mosiah handle the situation. It was his kingdom. Alma led the priests and their charges to Mosiah's palace. When Alma, his priests, the witnesses, and the prisoners were all inside, they filled the council hall. Mosiah, looking older, sat tiredly on his throne.

Alma approached him. Motioning to the prisoners, he said, "King Mosiah, we have brought before you these men and women who are accused by their brethren of having sinned against the Church. None of them are repentant of the sins they have committed. We bring them before you to judge them of their crimes."

Mosiah looked at the prisoners, then back at Alma. "Alma, unless these people have broken a civil law, I cannot judge them. If Church laws have been broken then the Church must judge them. As head of the Church you must be the judge."

With a sigh of resignation Alma looked at Mosiah. The king shrugged and smiled as if to say, I have given you total authority over the Church. Now use it.

Alma motioned to the priests and slowly they filed from the throne room with their prisoners.

Once outside, Gideon turned to Alma. "Now what do we do with these backsliders?"

Other priests gathered around waiting for Alma's answer. Alma held out his hands, palm up, and shrugged in a gesture of helplessness. "I don't know. I must inquire of the Lord."

He turned to Joshua. "Joshua, please take charge of the accused."

Alma turned and hurried down the street, leaving the large group of priests and prisoners standing before the palace. As he walked he thought about what he would do. He was pleased that he had turned over the prisoners to Joshua who was young and vigorous. Most of the priests were as old as he was. He made a mental note to ordain more young priests. But what of the prisoners?

Alma didn't return home but strode purposely through the city, out the gates, and down the familiar path into the forest. Now was one of those times when he needed to be alone in his prayers. When he reached his private glen, he knelt reverently on the damp earth.

"Father, I am troubled in my spirit," he prayed. "It is important to stop this apostasy, but now we have come this far, I am not sure what to do."

He prayed until the sun was far down its afternoon path. His knees were imbedded in the wet ground. He knew if he persisted the Lord would answer his prayers, and he was right.

The voice of the Lord came to him. *Blessed are you, Alma. And blessed are those whom you baptized in the Waters of Mormon.*

The voice continued, *you are blessed because of your great faith in the words of my servant, Abinadi. Your people are blessed because of their great faith in your words alone.*

Alma listened carefully as the voice of the Lord continued speaking to his mind. *Blessed are you, Alma, because of your diligence in establishing My church among this people. Blessed are the people of the church who take upon themselves My name, because they are Mine.*

You have inquired of Me concerning those who have transgressed My laws. Alma, you are blessed because you asked. Because you are my servant, I covenant with you that you shall be exalted. For now, though, continue to serve me by gathering together my sheep.

Alma found his voice. "Who are Thy sheep, Lord?"

He that will hear My voice shall be My sheep, and him you will receive into My Church if he believes in Me. Baptize the believers after they have repented, and I will forgive them.

For I will take upon myself the sins of the world. I have created all mankind, and everyone that believes in Me shall have a place at My right hand. But those who do not believe in Me shall come to stand before Me when the second trump shall sound. Then they shall know that I am the Lord their God, but they will not be redeemed but shall depart from Me into everlasting fire prepared for the devil and his angels.

A shiver went through Alma as he again thought of young Alma. Would his son be committed to everlasting fire? Then he reminded himself the Lord already promised that young Alma would be redeemed.

Exclude from the Church any who will not hear My voice. The Lord continued in his instruction. *Judge those in the Church who have transgressed. If they confess their sins and repent with full sincerity of heart, forgive them and let them remain in the Church.*

I will forgive people as often as they repent; you shall also forgive people their sins. I say unto you anyone who doesn't forgive another's sins when he repents is brought under condemnation.

Now go and judge those who have been brought before you. If they repent, forgive them and let them remain in My Church. If they do not repent they shall not be numbered among my people.

Alma knelt for a few more moments, then struggled stiffly to his feet. He shuffled through the forest, his mind reeling with all the Lord had told him. He could hardly wait to get it written down. At home, he greeted Esther and hurried to his library. Gathering paper, brushes and paint, he quickly recorded the Lord's words. Now he felt prepared to judge the people of the Church.

He hurried back to the palace. Faithful priests were still there. He led them to the Church where he rehearsed to them what the Lord said. Then, one by one, Joshua brought in the prisoners.

As each person stood before him the priest read the charges.

"Are you guilty of the charges?" was Alma's first question. Some answered with a defiant or sullen "Yes." For those who said nothing, Alma called for the testimony of the witnesses.

After determining guilt, Alma asked, "Before these witnesses, do you repent of these sins of which you are accused?"

In the entire afternoon, only one person confessed and begged forgiveness. She was a young woman taken in adultery. Alma felt she was truly penitent. As for the rest, Alma instructed the priests to blot their names from church records.

Alma looked at the unrepentant people before him. He shook his head sadly. He knew their fate. How could he convince them of their short-sightedness?

"Are you aware of what fate awaits you?" he asked.

No response.

"Are you prepared to face God in your unrepentant state?"

Still no response.

He waved to dismiss them. "Go," he said, his voice quavering. "Until you repent you are not welcome in the Church."

Watching them as they sidled out, tears welled in his eyes. "O, the cunning plan of the evil one. O, the vainness and the frailties and the foolishness of men," he whispered, "and they shall perish."

Alma sighed. "As you return to your churches," Alma said, "be prepared to judge others who have transgressed. Now is the time to purify the churches. The Lord has given us clear instructions."

As the witnesses and priests left the church, Alma said his goodbys. He loved these men. Each had been personally selected as priesthood bearers to govern churches in their scattered cities.

The repentant woman remained behind with Obadiah, the priest from Manti. Looking her in the eyes, Alma said, "Sister, the Lord has forgiven you. But from this time forth let no sin be part of you."

She stood on tiptoes and kissed him on the cheek. "Thank you. I have such a good feeling. I promise to sin no more."

Alma smiled, his eyes crinkling with pleasure. "That is good." He turned to the priest. "Obadiah, this sister will continue to be numbered among the people of your church. Watch over her—and them."

With the dissenters isolated and removed from the Church, peace and prosperity increased daily in the land. Alma spent his time regulating Church affairs. He was pleased with reports from cities of the numbers of people joining the Church and being baptized. Zarahemla had the greatest number of baptisms in any year since he had been there, not counting the baptism of the people of Limhi. Alma felt such joy.

Occasionally he would hear of Alma, his son. Never was there good news about him. Alma prayed daily that young Alma would come to his senses.

Alma was now seventy-two. He and his people had lived in the Land of Zarahemla for sixteen years. That would make young Alma almost thirty— "old enough to stop all of this foolishness," Alma muttered. His mind was troubled because he still had no successor— and he had already lived past the normal age of men. He thought of Obadiah and Joshua. Both were young enough and capable enough to take over the Church, but . . .

"I keep thinking of too many 'buts,' " he told Esther. "Each man has qualities that would make him a fine leader, but." Esther smiled. "See! There I go again."

Alma knew Esther was failing. During the past year she had not felt well enough to go with him on any of his travels. Now she was even unable to go for their regular evening walks. He was greatly saddened. She had been his joy and comfort for so many years. He silently prayed that when she died he could die soon after. Then again the recurring message hit him: I cannot die until I establish leadership in the Church.

"O Alma," he cried aloud. "Come back to the fold. I need you."

Alma stopped his traveling, trusting priests to administer to church affairs in the outlying cities. He devoted full time to Esther and the Church in Zarahemla. Day after day he watched as Esther became weaker. Her mind was still strong, but her body could no longer keep pace. Alma prayed that the Lord would let her live just a few more years. Physicians did their best but the time came when Esther's own remedies no longer helped.

* * *

Esther lay in the dark, her body tense, trying to suppress severe pains gripping her chest and arms. Finally she could stand the pain no longer. She moaned and sat up on the pallet.

"Alma."

She had only to speak his name once to arouse him.

He rolled over, surprised to see her sitting up. "What is it, my sweet?"

"Alma, I am in such great pain. I can no longer bear it. Please bless me."

He lighted the candle. Esther sat there exhausted, her breath coming in gasps. She tried to pray, but her pain was so severe she could hardly move her lips.

* * *

Alma knew from Esther's tone of voice that this was a major crisis. He could hear his own heart pounding. He laid his hands on her head and prayed aloud for her. As tears stained his weathered cheeks, he prayed the Lord would take away Esther's pain; that she could be at peace. After the prayer a calmness came upon him and he noticed the tension also drained from Esther. The Lord, showing His love for both of them, seemed in fill the room with his spirit.

* * *

Esther felt the pain begin to subside. Soon it was completely gone. "Thank you, Lord," she said softly. She took one of Alma's big hands in hers and squeezed it softly. He returned the squeeze. They lay there in silence, feeling the spirit, not wanting to break the spell by talking.

Finally Esther said quietly, "Alma, I think it is time." She shut her eyes, feeling she was drifting off to sleep.

* * *

Alma could not bear to let go of her hand. He relayed his messages of reassurance with finger tips, but finally there was no answering response. There surged through him a great feeling of the love of God, wave after wave, almost overwhelming him, as if the arms of the Lord were enfolding him, giving him peace and comfort.

He sat there until morning light filtered into the room. He was too stunned to weep. His wife, companion for these many years, was dead. He rose from the pallet. He must say farewell to this earthly shell of the woman he loved: goodby to the touch of her hand, her warmth, her compassion, her quiet reassuring smile. Thank goodness he had knowledge of the spirit world and the resurrection. He would not be long without his Esther.

* * *

Esther was buried with honors befitting a queen. She had been a devoted mate for over fifty years. Alma stood by her grave, knowing how much he would miss her. Beside her in her grave he put some of her favorite blankets and bowls, hoping these would represent a small token of his love.

Through tear-filled eyes he looked around at the people. Almost everyone he knew was there. King Mosiah and his brothers, Helorum and Helaman; Gideon and all of the priests; Helam's widow, Annah, and their children and grandchildren; his son, Zoram, with his wife, Micael. Zoram's daughter, Ma'Loni, and her children; both of his daughters, Netta and Leesa, with their husbands and children; and even his son, Alma.

Alma tried not to feel bitterness at what his youngest son had sought to do to him and the Church. But it had taken Esther's death to bring his rebellious son home. Four years had passed since he had seen the son who bore his name. He was shocked at the change. Young Alma's eyes, almost hidden by long unkempt hair and a full black beard, were lighted by the fire of religious zeal. He stood there silently aloof, watching the service.

After the burial was complete, Alma walked to him. "Alma, my son," he said, extending his hand in greeting. His son looked at him coldly, almost as if he didn't know him, then turned and walked away. Alma lowered his hand, his face contorted with grief. It is true, he thought. I have lost a wife to death, but worse yet, I have lost a son to apostasy.

* * *

Other than the gnawing in his stomach whenever he thought of young Alma, Alma's greatest sorrow was the growing separatism of the people of Zarahemla. The Church was strong—but so were the idol worshippers. They seemed to gain in numbers each day and now there were almost as many outside the Church as there were members. Persecutions against the Church of God increased almost daily.

Alma hoped that those not desiring to be members of the Church would just go their way and let the Church members alone. That was not the case. It seemed that those who dissented were not satisfied until they drew someone else with them.

"Isn't that the way with people," Alma mused, "to desire companionship in their miserable state. No one likes to sin by himself."

It seemed to Alma that after Esther's death, young Alma increased his antagonism and hatred towards the Church. Each day Alma was accosted by someone telling of the work of destruction in which Young Alma was engaged. It seemed his son was on a personal mission to destroy the Church.

"Why?" he kept asking himself. "Why does he try to destroy what I have worked so hard and long to build?"

Alma turned more and more to the scriptures. He soothed his soul with the psalms of David. He read the Lord's words which seemed to describe his own enigma:

I have found my servant; with my holy oil have I annointed him: with whom my hand shall be established: mine arm shall also strengthen him.

The enemy shall not exact upon him; nor the son of wickedness afflict him . . .

If his children forsake my law, and walk not in my judgments; If they break my statutes, and keep not my commandments; Then will I visit their transgression with the rod, and their iniquity with stripes.

Nevertheless my loving kindness will I not utterly take from from him, nor suffer my faithfulness to fail.

Alma read the psalm again, licked his dry lips, and whispered, "When, Lord?"

Regardless of negatives and persecutions, Alma continued instructing the people. He taught them to ignore afflictions imposed upon them, to walk in righteousness, serving the Lord in diligence. His instructions were to "pray without ceasing and give thanks in all things to the God who created you."

He followed his own advice. His nights were lonely without Esther, but his days were filled with earnest prayers for the Church, for the people, and for his son. His greatest personal goal—transcribing all the records onto gold plates—was about completed. Perhaps when that is done, he thought, and I have appointed someone to take my place as High Priest over the Church, perhaps then the Lord will permit me to join my Esther.

Chapter 13

Prayers of Faith Rewarded

"I know it is Church business," Alma argued, "but violence against people and property should also come under your jurisdiction. This matter is too serious to be considered only Church business."

Mosiah wearily leaned back in his chair. "Tell me once again what is happening."

Alma motioned to the runner from Melek. The lad, quite obviously awed to be in the king's chamber, came forward, his eyes on the rug. Hesitantly he told of Church members being beaten and left on the streets for dead, of rotten eggs and entrails of animals thrown on churches, of priests and teachers harassed and mocked as they walked the streets of the city, of noisemakers and chanters disrupting church services.

Nephihah, a teacher from Gideon, followed the Melek runner. He told of similar things happening in his city, adding that it was now impossible to hold a baptismal service because hecklers would find them, throw rocks, and cause such a commotion that people were afraid to meet.

Alma, white haired and balding, thanked them and turned back to Mosiah. "My king," he said in a firm voice. "These men represent Gideon and Melek. Runners from Manti, Sidom and Ammonihah report similar persecutions. People are being denied their right to practice their religion." Alma leaned closer to the throne. "Where is the freedom of which we have so often spoken. Is it only words?" Without realizing it, his voice had risen, quaking with emotion.

Mosiah shook his head. "No, my friend. You and I both know freedom is more than words. Freedom exists here under the laws of my father, and I am sworn to uphold those laws. I agree with you. Something must be done." He paused for a moment, then asked, "I know our sons are involved in this rebellion. How much?"

"I am afraid, Mosiah, that they are involved in teaching priestcraft for their own personal gain."

"Priestcraft?"

"Instead of following the wise counsel of your father, some teach that as priests they should be supported by the people." He continued sadly.

"My son, Alma, his friend Nehor, and your four sons are the chief advocates of this philosophy."

Mosiah nodded sadly. "I have been aware for some time that my sons were involved. What would you suggest we do?"

Alma took some time before answering, thinking of times when his own freedom had been forcibly taken from him. "I don't know what can be done, but I do know freedom of choice for our people may be lost, just as it was lost in the Land of Helam, and the Land of Nephi."

"I will not let that happen," Mosiah said seriously, "regardless of who is involved."

Alma's brow was furrowed as he continued his thoughts. "Freedom of choice is an everlasting principle. We as a people must have a climate in which religion can be nurtured." He looked at Mosiah. "If this persecution continues, those who are not strong in the faith will begin compromising their beliefs. Compromise leads to sin, sin leads to rebellion, and rebellion leads to apostasy and further persecution. This pattern has repeated itself numerous times. Many people will be hurt."

Mosiah nodded in agreement. "I can see that what you are saying is true. I will send forth a proclamation to all of my people."

"And?"

"The proclamation will insist upon freedom of choice. If necessary, we will use force of arms to enforce the proclamation."

"I hope it will not come to that," Alma said quietly, "but power of right may be necessary to overcome forces of evil."

Alma helped Mosiah draft the proclamation, which was sent to scribes for copying, then signed by Mosiah and sent to every city.

* * *

Netta, Alma's daughter, wandered through the square visiting with friends as they waited for the worship service to begin. In her hand she carried a bark paper containing a copy of the proclamation which Mosiah had sent out. She read it once more.

BE IT HEREBY KNOWN THAT NO ONE IN THIS LAND SHALL PERSECUTE ANOTHER FOR HIS BELIEFS. THE LAWS OF MY FATHER, BENJAMIN, CLEARLY STATE THAT THE PEOPLE OF THIS LAND SHALL HAVE FREEDOM TO CHOOSE THEIR BELIEFS, AS LONG AS THOSE BELIEFS DO NOT INFRINGE ON BELIEFS OF ANOTHER.

NO PERSON SHALL DENY THE RIGHT OF ANYONE TO BELONG TO ANOTHER CHURCH. THERE SHALL BE EQUALITY AMONG ALL MEN. LET NO PRIDE NOR HAUGHTINESS DISTURB THE PEACE OF THIS LAND. LET EVERY PERSON ESTEEM HIS NEIGHBOR AS

HIMSELF. LET EVERY MAN LABOR WITH HIS OWN HANDS FOR HIS
SUPPORT, INCLUDING ALL PRIESTS AND TEACHERS.

Those who surrounded Netta in the central temple plaza on the Sabbath discussed the proclamation. A priest, standing on the temple steps
began reading the proclamation. Netta didn't hear much of what he said.
She was too concerned about her father. She had watched as Alma seemed
to age rapidly after her mother died. Netta was concerned with the melan-
choly which now always seemed to be a part of him.

Her thoughts were interrupted,

"Alma, chief priest," the priest on the steps announced, "will speak to
us this day."

A hum went through the congregation. "The chief priest!" Much time
had passed since Alma last spoke. He had left teaching of the people to
other priests.

Netta watched as her father made his way up the temple steps to the
platform. He looked so frail.

Alma spoke of persecutions which had been directed against people
throughout the land. Then, his voice became animated. Netta thrilled at
the almost-forgotten eloquence of her father.

"Have we lost our sense of indignation?" he cried. "Are we so
selfsatisfied, so complacent, so preoccupied with enjoying our prosperity
that we blind ourselves to actions of those who would destroy that prosperity? Are these the people who fought to escape slavery of the Land
of Nephi and the Land of Helam to be free to worship their God according to their beliefs? Have we been hypnotized into a moral slumber? Let
us all examine our consciences and face our duty honestly and openly."

He continued quietly, "Those who teach priestcraft state openly that
conflict with the Church of God is a war which must be fought. They
cultivate some Church leaders while persecuting others, and even seek
to use religion as a means of personal gain. But they do not hide their
long-range plans. Those who are deceived about the essential conflict between priestcraft and religion are self-deceived."

He paused and then continued. Netta could see he was having a difficult time.

"One who leads the priestcraft movement, as most of you know, is my
own son." He lowered his eyes to the pavement. Then determinedly he
continued, his voice husky with emotion. "No person has the right to
persecute others for their beliefs—my son or anyone else. We believe in
freedom."

"Alma," he gestured eloquently, "has the right to choose to believe
whatever he desires, but he has no right to attempt to impose those beliefs
on others. Resist such teachings with your might. Battles are certain to
come, and battles will certainly be battles of ideas. Do not be complacent.

We have enemies now—remorseless, brutal, crude and cocky. Those enemies feel the Church of God is ripening for destruction. Prove to them otherwise."

His eyes roamed over the congregation, resting briefly on those he knew. "I have a personal request of you. As you must understand, I have prayed earnestly that my son, Alma, would repent of his evil ways and that he and those who follow him will return to the truth." He wiped a tear from his cheek with his forearm.

"I have become convinced it will take more than my prayers. I ask you to unite your prayers with mine, praying that Alma and those who persecute the Church will have a change of heart. Let us pray as a people until this comes to pass."

He slowly knelt on the stone platform. Netta, in the congregation, quickly followed his example, and soon everyone in the plaza was kneeling. Voices soon became a din as the prayers of hundreds of faithful church members rose on high.

* * *

An uneasy peace followed King Mosiah's proclamation. Alma was pleased. He noted with great satisfaction that the king's punishment was swift against any who persisted in persecuting the Church. He sent word to all his priests to continue to teach the words of King Benjamin in their churches. His message to the priests also asked that people continue to plead in their prayers that young Alma and his followers would repent and return to the Church.

As people prospered, they built new temples. In fact, it seemed to Alma that priests of various religions in the cities competed with each other to see who could build the highest and biggest temples. At least, he thought, temple building is a better outlet for competition than persecution.

New villages were established, and Alma ordained new priests and teachers for each community.

Alma, in his chambers at the Zarahemla temple, had just finished ordaining Zedekiah, a priest for the city of Zeezrom, when a loud commotion at the front of the temple disturbed him. He was upset that such noise would be allowed in his temple and he strode as quickly as he could to the entrance.

As Alma opened the door, he glanced down, then clutched at his chest and almost fell. Zedekiah caught and steadied him. There on the temple steps, lying as if he were dead, was his son, Alma. Surrounding him were the four sons of Mosiah.

Alma knelt at his son's side. There was an unearthly paleness about young Alma, accentuated by his pallid lips. There was no sign of life.

Alma's mind reverted back to the forest when Alma had lain before him just as helplessly after being attacked by the jaguar. Esther had been there then to help save his son. Alma's eyes brimmed. He had lost Esther and now it looked as though Alma, his son, was also dead. Alma put his ear close to his son's mouth and was thankful when he heard rasping sounds of labored breathing. At least he was still alive.

Alma looked up at Aaron, one of the sons of Mosiah, and asked quietly, "What has happened?"

Aaron shook his head, apparently unable to speak.

Ammon, another of Mosiah's sons, knelt beside him and placed his hand on Alma's bony shoulder. "I don't know how to tell you what happened. It is something beyond anything that I . . . " He looked up at his brothers, " . . . that we, have ever experienced." He stopped, apparently not knowing how to start.

Alma caressed his son's hair, looking anxiously at Ammon.

"We were traveling from Sidom to Gideon," Ammon began. "We were laughing, joking, and having a good time." He shook his head and swallowed hard as he remembered, "When . . . when . . . the earth started shaking beneath our feet, and . . . " Ammon stopped, as if he couldn't continue.

"And?"

Ammon again looked up at his brothers as if for moral support. "The earth shook and then a cloud seemed to cover us." He stammered again. "In the cloud was a shining person who looked like a man. He spoke to us."

Alma was completely absorbed. His eyes shone as he listened.

"His voice was like thunder."

"Well, what happened then?"

"We fell to the earth and hid our faces."

"What did the person say?"

"At first we didn't know what he said. We were so frightened we didn't understand even a word."

Alma was disappointed. "You mean you didn't understand him?" He looked down at his son, but young Alma still lay unconscious.

Ammon cleared his throat. "We did the second time he spoke."

Alma waited impatiently.

Himni, youngest of Mosiah's sons, handed Ammon a scroll. Ammon unrolled it as he said, "I don't think we will ever forget his words. But to make sure we don't forget, we wrote them down. "The angel said, 'Alma, arise and stand forth, for why do you persecute the church of God? For the Lord has said: *This is my church, and I will establish it; and nothing shall overthrow it, save it is the transgression of my people.*' "

Alma's heart beat excitedly in his chest. The Lord had answered his prayers and the prayers of his people! He was so choked with emotion he could hardly speak. His voice cracked as he asked, "Is that all the angel said?"

"No." Ammon continued reading from the scroll, "He said, 'Behold, the Lord has heard the prayers of his people, and also the prayers of his servant, Alma, who is your father . . . ' "

A sob escaped Alma's lips.

" . . . for he has prayed with much faith concerning you that you might be brought to a knowledge of the truth; therefore, for this purpose have I come to convince you of the power and authority of God, that the prayers of His servants might be answered according to their faith."

Alma clasped his hands before him, looking up at those circled around. "Praise the Lord," he whispered. Then he looked kindly at the bearded Ammon. "Please continue."

"And now behold," Ammon read, "can you dispute the power of God? For behold, does not my voice shake the earth? And can you not also behold me before you? Am I not sent from God?

"I say unto you, go. Remember the captivity of your fathers in the lands of Helam and Nephi, and remember what great things he has done for them, for they were in bondage and he has delivered them. And now I say unto you, Alma, go your way and seek to destroy the church no more, that their prayers may be answered, and this even if you will of yourself be cast off."

There was silence on the steps except for the faint and ragged breathing of his son who lay before him. Alma rejoiced at the goodness of God. God had actually sent an angel to bring young Alma to repentance!

"Were those the only words the angel spoke?" Alma asked quietly.

Ammon nodded.

"Then what happened?"

"We were so frightened and so astonished that we fell to the earth." Ammon shook his head in wonderment. "We saw an angel. With our own eyes we saw him."

Omner excitedly added, "And he did speak to us with a voice that sounded like thunder."

Aaron finally found his tongue. "And I know nothing but the power of God could shake the earth and cause it to tremble as though it would part asunder."

The other brothers nodded in agreement.

"But what happened to my son?"

Himni shrugged. "We don't know for sure. After the angel departed Alma tried to speak, but he couldn't. It was as if his mouth wouldn't even open."

"And he was so weak he fell to the earth," Ammon added. "We did our best to revive him, but nothing we did seemed to help. We made him comfortable, then took time to take our brushes and paper and write the words we had heard the angel speak. Then we picked up Alma and carried him here."

"It is enough," Alma said. He placed a hand on Ammon's shoulder. "Thank you." He looked at the other brothers, "It would be expedient that you go to the palace and tell your father what has happened. He has been concerned about you."

The brothers hung their heads. Ammon stood and the four brothers walked down the steps in the direction of the palace.

Alma tenderly took his son's hands in his own. He called Zedekiah and another teacher forward and had them carry young Alma into the temple. His son, dead to him for many years, now lived.

Turning to the temple priest, Alma said, "Send word for the people to gather." He motioned to Zedekiah, "Send runners to the churches in other cities. Have all the priests assemble here as quickly as they can. It is important that they hear my son's words when he returns to life."

The priests hurried to do his bidding.

Within hours, the temple plaza was filled. Alma stood before the crowd, his arms raised. When he had the people's attention he introduced the sons of Mosiah and had them rehearse all that had happened. Then they read the words of the angel. "An angel has spoken." Word spread like jungle fire to the furthest fringes of the crowd. There was pushing and shoving to get closer to hear.

Alma motioned to the priests. The younger Alma was carried out and laid on the steps.

"Before you now," he said, "you see the power of faith. The Lord has answered your prayers and mine."

* * *

From all quarters of the land priests assembled at the main temple in Zarahemla. They came because Alma had summoned them, but they also came because of their own curiosity. They wanted to see for themselves what had happened to young Alma and to speak with the sons of Mosiah.

There was some grumbling. "Why is it that we as faithful priests do not have an angel visit us, and these, who are unfaithful and enemies of the Church, are visited by an angel?"

That question was posed to Alma as he waited in the temple. He pondered for a moment, then looking at the priests before him, answered. "If an angel of the Lord appeared right now in this temple, standing in the air, filled with power and glory, I am sure we would all be greatly impressed. But, brethren, is it not true that each of you has felt promptings of the Spirit? Is it not also true that the Lord has spoken to you in your minds?"

Heads nodded.

"Brethren, each of you has been given the priesthood. Through that priesthood, you have power to communicate directly with the Father. You do not need angels to speak to you. Impressions of the spirit which we have received in our hearts are actually a higher form of revelation."

Joshua asked, "It seems to me the words of the angel would be more important."

"Let me illustrate my point with a familiar example from the scriptures," Alma replied. "In the story of Nephi, when he and his brothers went back to obtain the brass plates, do you not remember when the angel appeared to Laman and Lemuel?"

Gideon responded, "When they were in the cave hiding from Laban's men, and Laman and Lemuel began beating Nephi and Sam?"

Alma nodded. "Have you ever wondered why the angel appeared to the rebellious brothers and not to Nephi?"

They shook their heads.

"You see, Laman and Lemuel were not in tune with the spirit. An angel had to come to them to get through their senses. But Nephi conversed with the spirit often. Remember when Nephi was commanded by the spirit to slay Laban?"

The priests nodded.

"Nephi did not need an angel. He communicated directly through his spirit. Do you see which is the higher form of revelation?"

The priests seemed to understand.

Alma, pillow beneath his thin knees, knelt with other priests in the temple. For two days they fasted and prayed that young Alma would awaken. A shout aroused Alma from his prayer.

"He awakens!"

Opening his eyes, Alma looked down upon his son. It was true! Young Alma's eyes were open as he gazed around him. Alma put a hand under his son's neck, helping him sit up. Though very pale beneath his black beard, and still looking quite dazed, the youthful Alma looked at his father, a smile on his face. He winked one eye in a greeting that father and son hadn't shared since young Alma's childhood. Alma's heart sang within him.

Noticing his son's attempt to struggle to his feet, Alma motioned for two nearby teachers. Though shaky, Alma stood before the still-kneeling silent group of priests. His father stood beside him, lending not only physical but emotional support.

Young Alma spoke, softly at first, but his voice gained strength as he continued. "My brethren," he said, "be of good comfort. I thank you for your prayers in my behalf." He turned to his father as he continued, "Not only prayers you offer now for me, but prayers you have offered over the years that I might return to the truth."

His voice became filled with sureness. "I have repented of my sins and have been redeemed of the Lord." He looked around at the priests, many of whom he knew. "The Lord, in his mercy, has given me another chance. After much tribulation, even through repenting almost unto death, the Lord has snatched me out of everlasting burning which I had earned through my sins. Now I am born of God."

Young Alma put his arm around his father. "The Lord said, *Marvel not that all mankind must be born again; changed from their fallen state to a state of righteousness, being redeemed of God, becoming his sons and daughters. Thus they become new creatures. Unless they do this, they can in nowise inherit the kingdom of God.*"

He looked piercingly at those surrounding him. "Brethren, I testify to you that unless a person is born anew, he must be cast off. This I know, because I was about to be cast off." He looked at his father, then continued, "However, I have been redeemed from the gall of bitterness and bonds of iniquity. I was in the darkest abyss, but now I behold the marvelous light of God. My soul was racked with eternal torment, but now my soul is pained no more."

Alma had been holding his breath; his son's words were so exciting to him.

The younger Alma's voice dropped. "I rejected my Redeemer and denied those things which had been taught me by my father. Now I know that the Lord remembers every creature He has created and will manifest himself unto all."

He concluded, "I now know that all men shall stand before him to be judged at the last day, and that every knee shall bow and every tongue confess before Him at that time. All those who denied God in the world will confess that the judgment of an everlasting punishment is just upon them. They shall quake, and tremble, and shrink beneath the glance of his all-searching eye."

The hall was quiet as the younger Alma finished. No one spoke. No one shuffled his feet. The only movement was that of the scribe's brush recording young Alma's words. Everyone was awed by what he had said. The spirit witnessed to each of them that what had been spoken was true.

Alma put his arm around his son's neck. Wrinkled and leathery cheeks, pressed tightly to bearded ones, were dampened by mingling tears. Now priesthood succession was assured.

Chapter 14

Missionaries

The heaviness of silence lay between the two men. Alma looked at his son, now clean-shaven, seeing the image of what he, himself, had looked like at thirty. The younger Alma was dark and tall. His nose, though quite prominent, was not out of balance with his strong face.

Once more joy welled up in Alma's breast. He could see that young Alma, like himself, was buried in his own thoughts—thoughts of words spoken, of anger expressed, of hurts and anguish, thoughts of repentance, and tenderness, and love.

Young Alma broke the silence. "Father, I . . . "

Alma held up his hand. "My son, it is I who must speak first."

"No, father. I must ask forgiveness first of you. My heart is torn because of how I treated you and mother." He turned his face away and whispered, "Will I ever again feel peace in my heart?" Turning back, he said, "I look back over my life and all I can think of are times I was rebelling against you and your teachings. I know now by being in rebellion against you, I was in rebellion against God."

"Son, I . . . "

"Father, let me finish. As a child, I resented working and going to school to learn writing. It was not what I wanted to do. I learned to read and write, not because I wanted to, but because if I didn't you would punish me."

"Alma, . . . "

"And in Helam, when we were prisoners of Amulon and the Lamanites . . . " He looked at the floor. "I thought you were a coward because you wouldn't lift the sword against them." He wiped his arm across his face. "It was then I pulled away from you. Now I understand why you did what you did, but at that time I just couldn't respect a man who would let others push him around."

He looked at his father, then lowered his eyes. "At that time I didn't realize what real courage it took to remain silent and not fight back."

The white-haired Alma was silent.

His son looked up at him. "Then, when Ruth was taken and you did nothing about it, I vowed that as soon as I could, I would break away and never follow your leadership again."

He raised his hands in a gesture of helplessness. "I know now that in my heart I always secretly believed in God as you had taught me. Yet that belief was a part of you, and I wouldn't admit it, even to myself."

Alma could tell how painful this was for his son, but he remained silent now, wanting the whole story to be told; hoping that in telling, Alma would forgive himself.

Young Alma continued. "After cutting my emotional ties with you over what I then considered to be your cowardice, it was easy to cut my ties of belief in your God. All I needed was to find others with similar beliefs."

"But why the sons of the king?" Alma asked quietly.

"I hoped that leading them away might hurt you. I knew how close you were to Mosiah and thought that by hurting Mosiah I would hurt you." He looked at his father, pain showing in his eyes.

He gritted his teeth and looked down again. Continuing quietly but firmly, he said, "While my body was unconscious after the visit of the angel, my spirit was alert. I felt as if I were standing before the judgment seat. My life passed slowly before me. As each instance of my rebellion against you and God was shown to me, it was as if a hot knife were stabbed into my heart." He shook his head as he recalled those feelings. "I have never felt such anguish."

Alma waited.

"Father, I was pierced with eternal torment. My soul was tortured to the greatest degree by my knowledge of all my sins."

Alma remembered pain and torment he, himself, had gone through in the forest outside the City of Nephi when he had repented of his sins.

Young Alma stood. He paced the dimly-lighted room as he continued. "For what seemed an endless time, I prayed to God for forgiveness and for an end to my suffering. Peace did not come quickly. I continued in pain and torment in my spirit."

He stopped his pacing and stood before Alma. "Father, what troubles me most is through my influence, I the same as committed murder because I led many of our Father's children away to destruction." He sobbed and turned his face to the wall. "Thoughts of coming into the presence of God racked my soul with inexpressible horror."

He continued, "Father, thank you for teaching me about Jesus Christ. While I was tormented and wishing I could be banished, I remembered your prophecy concerning the coming of the Savior, and that He would atone for the sins of the world." He paused and swallowed several times, trying to control his emotions. "Though I had earlier denied Him, I prayed to Jesus that He would have mercy on me." He raised his shoulders eloquently, "Father, as soon as I prayed, my pain left me. Can you imagine the joy I felt?"

Alma could see a burning in his son's eyes. Young Alma spoke now with greater intensity. "The darkness around me started to disperse. A brilliant light seemed to burn around me. Then in that light I saw a radiant being. Then the Lord, for I determined it was He, spoke to me. I told you before most of the words He spoke, but there were others."

He paused, remembering. "He said every man must repent or suffer endless woe. He said those who would not repent would go forth with weeping and wailing and gnashing of teeth because of torment they would suffer. He commanded me to repent and obey the counsel of my father." He dropped down on his knees before his father.

Alma gazed down upon his son, seeing both anguish and joy in his eyes. He placed his hands on his son's shoulders.

"But that was not all, father. He also told me to repent or he would humble me with his almighty power. He told me to confess my sins or I would suffer the punishments of which He had spoken. Then He commanded me that for the rest of my earthly life I was to preach repentance to this people."

The younger Alma breathed deeply as he recalled the words of the Lord. "He promised me, father, that if I would do this—repent, confess my sins, and teach the people—I would have peace in my spirit once again."

Alma could only nod. His throat was choked so he could not speak. He took his son's hands in his and squeezed them.

"Father," words rushed out. "I saw a vision like father Lehi saw. I saw God sitting upon his throne, surrounded by concourses of angels singing and praising Him. I wanted with all my heart to be there, at His feet, praising Him." He paused, his eyes closed, as he remembered. "That's when I regained consciousness and saw you kneeling over me."

In a choking voice he asked, "Father, can you ever forgive me?"

Alma nodded again. A lump the size of his fist seemed in his throat so he still could not speak.

His son cradled his head on Alma's knees. "After suffering such anguish, after feeling such pain . . . " He sobbed. "Father, I really wanted to die and be banished, but I knew I couldn't die because I had not yet asked your forgiveness. I couldn't die until I had made an effort to right the wrongs I had committed against you, against God, and against the people of Zarahemla."

Alma let his breath out in a loud sigh. He reached out and encircled his son's neck, pulling him close, cradling him and rocking back and forth. "It is enough! It is enough!" he whispered into Alma's neck as tears scalded his eyes.

"My son, my son," Alma finally spoke. "All is forgiven. You have been lost and returned. My heart is full." He helped Alma to his feet.

"But, my son, I must also ask forgiveness of you." His voice quavered as he continued. "Please forgive me for the many occasions I did not give you my time. Forgive me for being so busy I didn't do things with you I should have done."

"You were doing the Lord's work."

"My son, that is no excuse to neglect those whom you love. Will you forgive me?"

"Of course."

Again they embraced, father and son of one name and now also of one heart.

Alma spoke softly to break the silence. "My son, do you remember the story of Joseph I told you when you were very young?"

"Our ancestor, Joseph, who was sold into Egypt?"

"Umm hmmm. I think I feel like Jacob, Joseph's father, must have felt."

"Refresh my mind about that part of the story."

Alma closed his eyes. He could almost picture Alma as a two-year-old on his lap as he told the story.

"After being sold into slavery by his brothers, Joseph was gone from his family for over twenty years. Jacob, his father, had given him up for dead. Then, during years of famine, when his brothers came for wheat, Joseph revealed who he was. Then he sent for his aged father. You can imagine Jacob's joy—to see again the son whom he had presumed dead." Alma's voice was husky. He cleared his throat. "My son, my feelings right now are similar to those Jacob must have felt. The son who was dead now lives."

* * *

The younger Alma departed Zarahemla with his friends, the sons of Mosiah, within a week after his return to consciousness. They all seemed driven to go back to the people they had led astray and preach to them the word of God.

Alma looked forward each week to his son's letters, usually newsy but brief. Young Alma wrote of people they met and of their preaching. Sometimes he included entire sermons. There was no mention of problems the missionaries were having, but whenever Alma visited with the king, Mosiah would tell him of persecutions which his sons wrote about. They had been beaten and mobbed but always the Lord pulled them through.

One of Aaron's letters mentioned Nehor. Alma recalled this man who had been his son's close friend during their growing-up years. Alma wrote to his son, "Is Nehor still preaching dissension? Has he not changed his ways to follow your teachings?"

Young Alma wrote back. "You ask about Nehor. He still leads opposition to our message. He has continued teaching of Zimpoc, the snake god, but I am convinced that he, like I was a few short months ago, is more interested in senines for Nehor than converts for Zimpoc."

Alma's letter continued. "We are exhorting people to keep God's commandments. In every city we confess the sins we have committed against the people. Then we tell them of the angel's visit and his words to us. We finish by bearing our testimonies that the Lord reigneth and it is He whom they should worship."

Alma saved each letter, and though his eyes were dim with age, he read and reread them. He was so proud of his son.

When the younger Alma came to Zarahemla to teach, the elder Alma went to listen. Young Alma delivered his sermon, calling the people to repentance lest they suffer "pains of the dark abyss which he had suffered."

Two years passed quickly, and soon the missionaries were home again. A short time later, the elder Alma was called to the palace. Netta, living with Alma since her husband died of the fever, walked with him. He was glad for her support.

Alma was ushered into the throne room. He looked around, seeing that Mosiah was obviously agitated. Young Alma, the four sons of Mosiah, and about a dozen additional men stood in the room. Alma recognized Muloki and Ammah, two of his son's converts.

He winked at his son, then smiled. The men in the room were those who had brought the unconscious Alma before him just two years before, but they looked different now. There was a different light in their eyes. And yes, he told himself, they are different people. They have literally been born again.

He came back to the present and smiled pleasantly at Mosiah. "What is it, my king?"

"It is my sons, that's what it is." sputtered the king. "I can't talk sense into any of them. I have asked that they stay in Zarahemla and help me administer the kingdom, but all they can talk about is missionary work."

Smiling again at the king's apparent irascibility, Alma asked, "What do you want of me?"

"Talk some sense into them." replied Mosiah.

Alma turned to the king's sons. "Tell me your desires," he said.

Ammon, the largest and most serious of the brothers, spoke, "Revered High Priest, Alma, for the past two years we have felt the joy of missionary work. We have paid for our wickedness by teaching the people of Zarahemla about the true God. We would like to leave the rest of the teaching to the priests whom you have appointed."

Alma nodded. That sounded reasonable enough. "Go on."

"We have asked our father," Ammon nodded towards the frowning Mosiah, "to grant permission for us to go to the land of Nephi so we can preach to our Lamanite brothers."

Alma looked from Ammon back to the king. Mosiah nodded.

Ammon continued. "We desire to bring them to knowledge of the Lord. Perhaps we can cure them of their hatred towards the Nephites."

"And through the knowledge we teach them of God, perhaps we can help them avoid further fighting and contention," added Omner excitedly.

Aaron, oldest and most quiet of the brothers spoke up. "We are desirous that salvation should be preached to every creature. We cannot bear to think that any human soul should perish." His eyes misted. "Even the thought of people having to undergo endless torment is of great sorrow to us."

"So," Ammon ended, "we have asked our father to allow us to go teach the Lamanites. But," he shrugged, "he won't listen to our plea."

"What can I do?" Alma asked.

"Pray to the Lord to see if I should let them go," interjected Mosiah. "You are the high priest and this is a religious matter. I feel we need the Lord's word."

"You are the seer, however," Alma said, his eyes twinkling at Mosiah's obvious discomfiture.

"This is something I want you to do," the king said, ignoring Alma's levity.

Alma nodded. "I will inquire of the Lord." He motioned to Netta. Together they walked from the hall. As they moved along the street, Alma said. "My dear, I desire to go into the forest to pray, but it has been some time since I had energy to do so. Will you help me?"

They walked slowly down the forest path to the glen where Alma had spent so much time in earnest prayer. "Please stay with me," he instructed his daughter.

He knelt on the ground, praying silently at first, then opening his mouth to the Lord. "Father, please tell me what Thou desirest of these young men. I pray not only for the sons of Mosiah, but for Alma also. What is Thy will?"

He nodded as the inner voice told him what he should tell the king.

Silently, he and Netta walked back to the palace. Darkness settled around them as they made their way through broad streets. Torches blazed brightly on palace walls. Servants led them into the throne room. Alma walked slowly forward and stood directly before Mosiah's throne.

"The Lord has spoken to me concerning this matter," he said.

"Well, what did He say?" asked Mosiah in a voice tinged with irritability.

"The Lord said, *Let them go up, for many shall believe on their words, and they shall have eternal life; and I will deliver thy sons out of the hands of the Lamanites.*"

An excited chatter passed around the room. Mosiah nodded tiredly. "Yes, I thought that was what He said." He shrugged. "If it is to be, it is to be." He turned to his sons. "When would you want to depart?"

"As quickly as possible," Aaron said.

"But what of the kingdom?" Mosiah asked. "I am an old man. Which of you will be king?"

"Not I," the sons answered in chorus.

* * *

Alma looked over those who had chosen to depart on this mission: Ammon, Aaron, Omner, Himni, Muloki and Ammah and several others he had seen but did not know their names. All stood now on the temple steps, illuminated by hundreds of torches stuck in niches around the building. A huge crowd filled the square. Some were curious about those going to the land of the Lamanites. Others were friends and relatives. A spirit of rejoicing was in the air. This was the first time anyone had gone on such a mission since King Mosiah had sent the other Ammon and his party to find the land of Nephi, which had resulted in Limhi and all of his people escaping to Zarahemla.

Alma blessed each of the missionaries and set them apart for their work. He prayed their efforts would be as rewarding as that of the earlier Ammon; through their missionary work, they, too, would bring a people to salvation.

The younger Alma stood dejectedly on the steps. He had also wanted to go, but his father had restrained him.

"My son, I am past the age when most people die. My eyes are dim and my hands are shaky. I can no longer keep the records of this people. The Lord wishes you to be my hands and eyes."

"What do you want me to do?"

"Since Nephi's time, someone has been responsible to keep the history of the people. We must write down God's dealings with our people so future generations may learn from our experiences. I need you to be that chronicler."

"I will do it, father."

Alma didn't add that he was also ready to ordain his son as high priest. That would wait for another day—hopefully when his son was married. Responsibility as scribe would be a training ground for the future high priest.

On the day Ammon and young Alma's other friends left for their mission to the land of Nephi, the new scribe wrote, "It has been five hundred and one years since Lehi left the land of Jerusalem."

* * *

A year had passed since Mosiah's sons had gone to the Land of Nephi. The elder Alma kept very busy completing the records. Most of his time was spent in the palace library. He was there this day, deep in thought, sitting in the palace archives, when his son burst in.

"Father," the younger Alma cried.

"What is it, son?"

Composing himself, young Alma said, "Father, remember Helam's daughter, Ruth, who was taken by the Lamanites?"

Alma nodded.

"She is here!" his son almost shouted.

"What? How could that be?" Alma rubbed his eyes which were sore from reading. "It has been . . . " He took a moment to calculate. " . . . it has been almost twenty years."

"I know, father. Aaron discovered her and the other Nephite women in the temple at Nephi. He received permission from the Lamanites to send them home along with letters for you and Mosiah."

"Letters?"

"Yes, father. Aaron and the other sons of Mosiah have been very successful converting the Lamanites. And they have sent Ruth home." His son grabbed him by his hand and almost pulled him into the throne room. Mosiah sat there, several scrolls on his lap. He looked up as Alma and his son approached.

"They are all safe and well," the king said, a huskiness in his voice.

"Just as the Lord promised," Alma smiled.

"Yes," Mosiah nodded, "just as the Lord promised. Aaron sends you greetings. They have many converts including several of the Lamanite Kings."

Alma shook his head in wonder. "Even kings," he mused. He looked at Mosiah. "Alma tells me that the women . . . "

Mosiah interrupted, "Yes, they sent the Nephite women back with an escort. Ruth and the others served as priestesses for all of these years in Lamanite temples. I sent them to their homes for a reunion with their parents."

Alma nodded sadly, "Oh, if only Helam were still alive to see his daughter again."

* * *

Alma celebrated his seventy-sixth birthday by uniting young Alma and Ruth in marrige. It was a simple ceremony, attended by relatives and a few friends. Alma rejoiced in the light of love he saw in Alma's eyes. His son had waited many years. Ruth was still a beautiful woman. Her long black hair, parted in the middle, hung low on her back. She had full lips, tinted now with berry juice. Her eyes were large and expressive. She would be a fine wife for his son.

As Alma watched the honeymoon preparations, he rejoiced, also, in one other way. Ever since his son's conversion, he had pleaded with him to find a mate. He had refrained from ordaining young Alma as high priest until he married. Now that problem was settled. Alma and Ruth would settle down in a home of their own, and he would call his son, Alma to the holy calling of High Priest.

Chapter 15

Twenty-Four Gold Plates

"I think I know how you feel." Alma was empathetic. "I have had a similar situation."

"I am so frustrated," Mosiah said.

Alma leaned back with a feeling of satisfaction. "For years my greatest worry was who would succeed me as high priest. But that problem was solved. Thank the Lord that my son came back. He makes a fine high priest."

"But Alma, my brothers, Helaman and Helorum are dead. Ammon, Aaron, Omner and Himni are in the land of Nephi teaching the Lamanites. Who does that leave to succeed me?"

"Perhaps your sons will be back by the time you desire to turn over the kingdom."

Mosiah turned to the window, not answering, then said quietly, "I am ready now. Besides, I don't think I have that much time." He looked at his friend. "You have lived an extremely long life. I am already past man's normal life span." He shuddered. "This last year the fever has kept me in bed much of the time." He lapsed into thought again, then said, "Alma, what will happen if I die without a successor to the kingship?"

Alma shook his head. "With the dissension we already have in the Church and in the land, there would be chaos. Many would strive to be king. There would be contention and fighting."

Mosiah nodded. "So what am I to do?"

"Are you asking my advice?"

"Yes," Mosiah said impatiently. "You are my advisor. You are close to the Lord. I need some help thinking this through."

Alma was thoughtful. "I would say that the first thing to do is to get all the affairs of the kingdom in order."

"They are in order."

Alma leaned forward, a serious look on his face. "Mosiah," he said, "I know that right now you are concerned about what will happen to the kingdom. So am I, but I am more concerned about the records."

"In what way?"

"For more than twenty years we have had scribes inscribing the records onto gold plates. What will happen to the records and relics when we die?"

Mosiah thought for a moment, then shook his head. "I don't know. No one has been given responsibility for them."

Alma scooted his stool closer to the king. "Mosiah, my friend. You have been a great king. We have had almost continual peace under your leadership. May I make a suggestion?"

Mosiah shrugged.

"Who had the plates prior to your father's reign?

"The large plates of Nephi have always been with the kings."

"And the small plates?"

Mosiah paused before answering. "The small plates were given to my father by Amaleki, the last Nephite scribe."

Alma leaned back. "You remember that the Lord instructed Nephi to keep both sets of plates, and that the plates would someday be used to convert our descendants and the gentiles. If you died now, the records might be lost."

"What are you suggesting?"

Alma spoke intently. "Turn them over now to Alma. Put them back in the hands of the Lord's priesthood. As high priest, he will keep and preserve the records for posterity."

"Both sets?"

"There has been only one set of records kept since your grandfather's time."

Mosiah didn't answer for some time. Finally he looked at Alma. "I suppose that it must be." He sat, chin on chest, thinking, then roused himself, "Before I turn over the plates, there is one more thing to do."

"What?"

"The twenty-four gold plates brought by King Limhi's people; they must be translated."

Alma nodded.

"Will you help me?"

"Of course, but you are the seer. You have the interpreters."

"But the translation will take both of us. I will translate if you will record."

"Agreed."

* * *

The next months were exciting for Alma. He had prepared himself to die but now had renewed purpose to live. He thrilled as he wrote the story recorded on the twenty-four plates. Sometimes he became so engrossed in what Mosiah read that he forgot to write, then had to have words repeated.

He was amazed at the faith of Jared's brother. Alma reread the words of the brother of Jared he had just written:

"I know, O Lord, that thou hast all power, and can do whatsoever thou wilt for man's benefit; therefore touch these stones, O Lord, with thy finger, and prepare them that they may shine forth in darkness . . . "

Alma nodded his head in admiration. In this example, faith was not shown in asking the Lord how to light the ships, but in presenting the stones for the Lord to touch!

Even more exciting for Alma was the story of Jared's brother actually seeing the Lord. Many times the Lord had spoken to Alma; many times Alma had felt the comfort given by the Holy Ghost. Now, as he read the story he was writing, he yearned to see his Lord as the brother of Jared had done.

Alma read again the brother of Jared's request that the Lord reveal himself. He wondered if he would be so brave: to ask the Lord for such a thing! He continued reading where the Lord asked if Jared's brother believed His words. The brother answered affirmatively. Alma read,

"And when he had said these words the Lord showed himself unto him, and said: *Because thou knowest these things ye are redeemed from the fall; therefore ye are brought back into my presence; therefore I show myself unto you. Behold I am he who was prepared from the foundation of the world to redeem my people. Behold, I am Jesus Christ.*"

Alma sat back, brush in hand. "Another witness for Christ," he breathed softly. He turned to Mosiah who was waiting to continue. "How can some men not believe in the Savior's coming?" he asked.

Mosiah smiled. "Wasn't there a time in your own youth when you didn't believe?"

Alma responded with a shrug. "Father taught about the Lord, but I really never listened until I heard Abinadi's prophecies. I finally understood Isaiah's words." He continued quietly. "Since then I have read the testimony of Lehi who had seen the Lord in vision, and Nephi who had seen the Lord and spoken to him, and Jacob, and Enos. Now add the testimony of the Brother of Jared."

"And in your own life?" Mosiah suggested.

"I cannot begin to name the times the Lord has spoken to me and confirmed the words of the prophets."

* * *

The translation continued day after day. Mosiah translated, Alma wrote: the journey across the great waters; boats being actually buried in the water; landing and settling of the land by Jared's people.

Alma stopped Mosiah as he read of the Jaradites first attempts at government. "Read again that last part."

Mosiah read through the interpreters, "The people desired that they should anoint one of their sons to be a king over them."

"Go on."

"And this was grievous unto them. And the Brother of Jared said, 'Surely this thing leadeth into captivity.' "

"That's far enough."

Mosiah looked at Alma inquisitively.

Alma struggled, trying to find the right words. "My friend, perhaps Jared's words will help you in your decision."

"What do you mean?"

"You have been concerned about passing on the kingship. If the brother of Jared is right—that having a king might lead into captivity—you have the opportunity to make some decisions which will greatly affect our people's future."

Alma continued, ticking each point off on his fingers.

"Nephi taught there should not be kings upon this land."

Mosiah nodded.

"Because of wicked King Noah, I and all my people could have been lost had we not listened to Abinadi."

Mosiah nodded again.

"Now the brother of Jared speaks out against having a king."

Alma leaned closer. "Mosiah, perhaps the Lord created this situation to help you make a decision to abolish the kingship." He sat quietly, anticipating Mosiah's response.

The king closed his eyes in contemplation, rocking gently back and forth. "Perhaps you are right, but I am unsure what form of government would work for this people. I will have to do more thinking," he said. "Let us return to our translating."

Mosiah read and Alma wrote of King Orihah and his righteous reign, of his sons and the rebellions which began with his grandson. Alma could see that the Brother of Jared's prophecy about having a king leading people into captivity was taking place. He hoped that Mosiah was also thinking about what he was translating.

Tears dimmed his vision as he wrote of wars and persecutions and trials. The record was one of continuous strife and bloodshed. Even when people had a rightous king, his reign would only last a few years until warfare would again erupt.

As days of translating lengthened into weeks, Alma wondered how a people could handle so much war, so much contention. Then he realized that must be why they were eventually destroyed. What a waste: to deteriorate from a righteous people until the Lord totally destroyed them because of wickedness. As the translation continued, that feeling was borne out when he read of countless prophets that came to the people during the days of Com, calling people to repent or they would be destroyed. Alma nodded. Their prophecies had come true even though the people had rejected them.

Finally the record told of Ether and his writings. Ether must have been a man of faith like the Brother of Jared. As Mosiah translated, the earth's story unfolded before them. Ether wrote of the creation, the Garden of Eden, and all things down to their own time. He spoke of this land as the chosen land. Alma thrilled at Ether's description of the promised land and how this land would continue to be a chosen land as long as the people who dwelled upon the land should serve God. Alma put his brush down and sat thinking about the future.

He looked at Mosiah. "Ether spoke of a new heaven and a new earth. I wonder when that will be?"

"Ether also spoke of a New Jerusalem coming from heaven in the last days which would be placed in this land," Mosiah added.

"I continue to be amazed," Alma said. "Read to me again about the New Jerusalem."

Mosiah read slowly through the two stones, "And then cometh the New Jerusalem; and blessed are they who dwell therein, for it is they whose garments are white through the blood of the Lamb; and they are they who are numbered among the remnant of Joseph's seed, who were of the house of Israel."

"Ether lived hundreds of years before Father Lehi and his people came to this country, and yet, he foretells the future as if he were already there."

"Even to seeing the days of the Savior," said Mosiah.

Alma listened as Mosiah read Ether's predictions concerning the Old Jerusalem and the gathering of the Jews. He shuddered as Mosiah translated the last page which told of the once mighty people's destruction and the final battle between Shiz and Coriantumr.

For more than two months he and Mosiah had spent every day in translation. They had recorded a people's history from the time of the great tower; crossing the ocean, deterioration from righteousness to unrighteousness; and finally their destruction.

Mosiah translated and Alma carefully wrote Ether's final words.

"Whether the Lord will translate me or whether I die won't matter, if it so be that I am saved in the kingdom of God."

Alma put his brush down, his heart heavy. Ether had expressed his own desire. I am ready to die, too, he thought. My affairs are now in order. Alma, my son, has been ordained High Priest. I just want to join Esther and my Lord in the paradise of which Nephi had spoken.

He thought of Jared's people. Why? Why wouldn't people listen to the Lord's prophets? Why did people choose evil over good? Why? Why? Why? He sat there, immersed in thought; troubled because similar wickedness was in his own people. He silently prayed, When, O Lord, will all people turn to Thee and follow Thy word?

His thoughts were interrupted by Mosiah's quiet voice.

"I have made a decision."

Alma looked at Mosiah. The king looked out the window, hands clasping and unclasping before him.

"I have decided that having a king is not wise for our people."

Alma waited for Mosiah to continue.

Mosiah looked at Alma, his eyes filled with agony that could not be expressed verbally. The king shook his head. "I hope that our people will never come to such destruction as we have just read about. If renouncing the kingship will help prevent that destruction, then I will renounce the kingship."

Leaning heavily on his cane, Alma shakily rose to his feet, walked to Mosiah and leaned over him.

"My friend, I feel that the Lord is pleased with your decision."

* * *

The next weeks were busy ones. Alma's activities belied his eighty-one years. Mosiah had assigned him the task of transferring the records and he devoted heart and soul to the task.

With Mosiah's permission and encouragement, he had scribes make many bark paper copies of the translation of the twenty-four gold plates. These he distributed to the people, hoping they would serve as a warning to shun all wickedness.

He assigned scribes to copy the Jaredite records to gold plates so they would be preserved for future generations. Several months were thus occupied as he carefully supervised the inscribing. Finally, the project was done. Regardless of what happened to paper copies of the records, all writings were now permanently inscribed on gold plates which would last thousands of years until the Lord in his wisdom might use them in teaching another people.

He reported to the palace. King Mosiah was there with scribes, writing and rewriting concepts of how the people should be governed. Mosiah greeted Alma with a tired smile.

"The inscriptions are completed," Alma said.

"Every record on plates?"

Alma nodded.

Sighing, Mosiah said, "Then we are ready. Have your son, Alma, come to the palace when the sun is at midpoint in the afternoon."

"It shall be done."

As Alma left the palace, he thought how tired Mosiah looked. He glanced up at the heavens. "Lord, please let us live long enough to take care of the records and the governance of this people."

A calm feeling permeated his being. "Thank you, Lord," he whispered.

* * *

In mid-afternoon, Mosiah and the two Almas met in the palace library. Mosiah walked around the room, gently touching the case holding the brass plates, Laban's sword, the Liahona, the twenty-four plates he and Alma had just translated, and each of the stacks of plates on the shelves.

Turning to the younger Alma he said, "Treasures in this room represent all of God's dealings with man from the beginning."

Both Alma's nodded. Alma felt a lump rise in his throat.

Mosiah continued, "I am a king, not a prophet, yet I have seen in vision that these records represent salvation for millions of people who will read them and come to a knowledge of the Savior."

He picked up the small plates of Nephi and gently fondled them. "Nephi wrote that 'wherefore the Lord God will proceed to bring forth the words of the book; and in the mouth of as many witnesses as seems good will he establish his word; and wo be unto him that rejects the word of God!' "

He walked to the younger Alma and placed the plates in his hands. "The Lord said that through these plates and these records, *I will proceed to do a marvelous work among this people, yea, a marvelous work and a wonder, for the wisdom of their wise and learned shall perish and the understanding of their prudent shall be hid."*

Mosiah continued to look the younger Alma in the eye. "Through these records those who have erred will come to understanding, and they that murmured will learn the Lord's doctrine.

"Alma, you have been ordained as High Priest over this people. Your father and I both feel that as High Priest you should be custodian of these records. I confer them upon you: records, interpreters, and all the relics of our people."

"I am overwhelmed," Alma said.

"I command you that you shall keep and preserve them throughout your life, and when the time comes for you to die, you are to confer them onto a righteous priesthood holder who will carry on the records."

"I will do so humbly," he said.

"Not only are you responsible for preserving these records," Mosiah continued, "but you are commanded to also keep a record of this people."

"That I am already doing." He turned to his aged father. "Now I see your wisdom and the Lord's purposes in the scribe's training which you insisted I take as a youth."

Alma could not speak. His throat was constricted and his eyes burned. He was pleased at the younger Alma's reaction. He knew of the younger Alma's love for the sacred records; of the time young Alma spent in the palace library researching material for sermons and copying records onto paper scrolls for use in teaching the people.

The new High Priest continued, eyes mirroring his feelings. "I have dedicated the remainder of my life to the Lord's work. I will treasure and preserve His records. I will be His scribe."

Chapter 16

A Government of the People

Alma and Mosiah sat alone in the anteroom behind the throne room. The king's eyes were bloodshot. Dark circles under them accentuated his look of tiredness.

Mosiah handed Alma a paper. "This is my first draft of the proclamation. Please read it."

The paper fluttered in Alma's shaking hands. He read the first paragraph.

BEHOLD, MY BRETHREN, FOR I ESTEEM YOU AS SUCH, I KNOW YOU DESIRE TO HAVE A KING. HE TO WHOM THE KINGDOM RIGHTLY BELONGS HAS DECLINED TO BE KING OVER YOU. IT IS HIS DESIRE, RATHER, TO BE A TEACHER AND A MISSIONARY.

Alma looked up.

Mosiah nodded, "Go on."

I AM CONCERNED THAT IF I APPOINT ANOTHER IN HIS STEAD THERE MIGHT BE CONTENTION IN THE LAND. PERHAPS OUR PEOPLE WOULD FIND THEMSELVES AS THE JAREDITES, FIGHTING WITH ONE ANOTHER FOR THE KINGDOM, WITH WAR AND SHEDDING OF MUCH BLOOD WHICH WOULD PERVERT THE WAY OF THE LORD AND WOULD DESTROY THIS PEOPLE.

Alma nodded his head in affirmation. "Mosiah, you show great insight."

He continued reading.

NOW I SAY UNTO YOU, LET US BE WISE AND CONSIDER WHAT WE ARE DOING. WE HAVE NO RIGHT TO DESTROY MY SON OR ANY OTHER WHO WOULD BE APPOINTED AS KING. WHAT WE ALL DESIRE IS PEACE FOR THIS PEOPLE.

"Your words will inspire the people." Alma read on.

IT IS BETTER THAT A MAN SHOULD BE JUDGED OF GOD THAN OF MAN. JUDGMENTS OF GOD ARE ALWAYS JUST, BUT JUDGMENTS OF MAN ARE NOT ALWAYS JUST. IF IT WERE POSSIBLE THAT YOU COULD HAVE JUST MEN TO BE YOUR KINGS, WHO WOULD ESTABLISH THE LAWS OF GOD AND JUDGE THIS PEOPLE ACCORDING TO HIS COMMANDMENTS, AND IF YOU COULD HAVE MEN

FOR YOUR KINGS WHO WOULD DO EVEN AS MY FATHER, BEN-JAMIN, DID FOR THIS PEOPLE, THEN YOU COULD ALWAYS HAVE KINGS TO RULE OVER YOU.

Alma read further into the proclamation as Mosiah listed the strengths of his thirty-two years as king of Zarahemla. Mosiah listed such things as establishing and maintaining peace throughout the land, of punishing criminals according to the laws of the land.

Mosiah wrote that if all men were just, there would be no problem having a king. He then used King Noah as an example of what an unrighteous king can do.

Alma nodded in agreement, rubbed his tired eyes, and turned back to the proclamation.

WHAT GREAT DESTRUCTION CAME UPON KING NOAH AND HIS PEOPLE. BECAUSE OF THEIR INIQUITIES THEY WERE BROUGHT INTO BONDAGE. IF IT WEREN'T FOR THE KINDNESS OF A JUST AND ALL-WISE CREATOR AND THEIR OWN SINCERE REPENTANCE THEY WOULD STILL BE IN BONDAGE. BUT THE LORD DID DELIVER THEM BECAUSE THEY DID HUMBLE THEMSELVES AND DID CRY MIGHTILY UNTO HIM. THUS DOES THE LORD WORK WITH HIS POWER AMONG THE CHILDREN OF MEN, EXTENDING THE ARM OF MERCY TOWARDS THEM THAT PUT THEIR TRUST IN HIM.

"Well said," Alma remarked.

BUT WHAT WOULD HAPPEN TO YOU IF YOU SHOULD HAVE A WICKED KING? YOU COULD NOT DETHRONE HIM WITHOUT CONTENTION AND THE SHEDDING OF BLOOD.

"Very true," Alma whispered. He then read on, where Mosiah talked about any wicked king having friends in his iniquity. Such a king, he said, would trample all righteousness and would enact laws to further his own wickedness. Anyone who disobeyed these laws or rebelled would be destroyed.

AND SO WOULD AN UNRIGHTEOUS KING ALWAYS PERVERT THE WAYS OF RIGHTEOUSNESS. MY PEOPLE, I DO NOT DESIRE THAT SUCH ABOMINATIONS SHOULD COME UPON YOU.

Alma put down the proclamation. "You have presented the case extremely well." He tapped the paper. "This proclamation should convince your people. Now, what have you proposed to take the place of the kingdom?"

Mosiah handed another paper to Alma. "See what you think of this," he said.

I WILL REMAIN YOUR KING FOR THE REST OF MY DAYS, BUT IN THE MEANTIME LET US APPOINT RIGHTEOUS JUDGES TO JUDGE THIS PEOPLE ACCORDING TO THE LAWS OF THE LAND AND THE COMMANDMENTS OF GOD.

Alma looked up. "Who will you appoint as judges?"

Smiling tiredly, Mosiah replied. "Please read on."

Alma nodded and continued reading.

I, YOUR KING, PROPOSE THAT YOU CHOOSE JUDGES BY THE VOICE OF THE PEOPLE, THAT YOU MAY BE JUDGED ACCORDING TO THE CORRECT LAWS WHICH HAVE BEEN GIVEN YOU. LET THE PEOPLE RULE BY MAJORITY VOTE, FOR SELDOM WILL THE MAJORITY DESIRE ANYTHING THAT IS CONTRARY TO THAT WHICH IS RIGHT.

IF THE TIME EVER COMES THAT THE MAJORITY OF THE PEOPLE CHOOSE INIQUITY, THEN IS THE TIME THAT THE JUDGMENTS OF GOD WILL COME UPON YOU. THEN IS THE TIME GOD WILL VISIT YOU WITH GREAT DESTRUCTION EVEN AS HE HAS DONE BEFORE IN THIS LAND.

Alma set the proclamation down. He asked Mosiah, "What procedures have you outlined in case a judge proves to be unrighteous?"

"That is one of the reasons I asked you here," Mosiah replied. "I wanted you to read what I prepared, but I need help setting up procedures for removal of unrighteous judges."

Alma sat back steepling his hands before him.

He mused, "Will judges be of the same rank, having similar responsibilities?"

"I envision setting up the judgeship similarly to how you have set up the priesthood. A chief judge would preside over the entire land, then there would be lesser judges in each city."

Alma nodded. "That would work."

"If a lesser judge were unrighteous, then the chief judge could simply remove him from office."

"True."

"My main problem comes with what to do if the chief judge proves to be unworthy. What provisions exist for removal of the high priest?"

Alma smiled at the king. "Hopefully, that problem would never exist. But yes, such provision has been made. Priests of each city could unite together in a vote and depose any unrighteous high priest."

Mosiah called, "Samuel!"

A scribe came into the room, carrying several rolls of paper, some brushes and paint.

"Please write," Mosiah said. He stood by the window, his hand on his chin.

Alma watched, pleased that such a righteous king had been called to govern this people. He listened as Mosiah dictated what they had just discussed concerning the removal of unrighteous judges.

When Mosiah finished, Alma said, "Good. Not only have you established who should govern the land, but you have established guidelines which keeps power in the people's hands."

Mosiah dictated to the scribe his trials as king. He told of attempting to judge all people fairly, of travails of soul as he listened to complaints and concerns of people. He commented on his hurts at the murmurings and contention of the people.

"It is not right," he dictated, "That one man, your king, should bear this heavy burden. Governing this land should be the responsibility and obligation of all people."

Mosiah recalled for the people the story of the Jaredites, of their contention and wickedness because of having evil kings. He commented on ambitions of men who would desire to be king and to control the people. Such ambitious men would lead the people into unrighteousness and take advantage of them. He enumerated for them the problems of having a wicked king:

"They would suffer his iniquities and abominations.

"There would be wars and contentions and bloodshed.

"Evil would rule the land. There would be stealing and plundering and committing of whoredoms.

"They would be heavily taxed to support the king and his followers.

"An unrighteous king would not work for himself, but would expect the people to work for him and support him."

Mosiah told how civilization which was established would collapse if spiritual values, moral stamina, or people's responsibility declined. Such collapse would also come if a king imposed severe controls over the people.

Alma agreed with all Mosiah had written. When the proclamation was completed, he read.

I COMMAND YOU TO DO THESE THINGS IN FEAR OF THE LORD. I COMMAND YOU THAT YOU NO LONGER HAVE A KING TO RULE OVER YOU. THEREFORE, EACH OF YOU IS ACCOUNTABLE. IF YOU COMMIT SINS AND INIQUITIES, THEY SHALL BE ANSWERED UPON YOUR OWN HEADS.

I DESIRE THAT THERE SHOULD BE NO INEQUALITY THROUGHOUT THIS LAND. I DESIRE THIS LAND TO BE A LAND OF LIBERTY, A LAND WHERE EVERY MAN MAY ENJOY HIS RIGHTS AND PRIVILEGES ALIKE, SO LONG AS THE LORD SEES FIT THAT WE MAY LIVE AND INHERIT THE LAND—EVEN AS LONG AS ANY OF OUR POSTERITY REMAINS UPON THE FACE OF THE LAND.

Alma finished reading, laboriously got to his feet and crossed over to Mosiah. He put his arms around him, hugging him tightly.

"I don't know if this is appropriate behavior for one of your subjects, Mosiah, but I want you to know my feelings. What you have done today will set standards of government until the Savior comes and establishes his heavenly kingdom."

* * *

"Would you like more chocolate, Father?"

Alma nodded. Being home and visiting with his son gave him great joy. The younger Alma poured honey in the cup, stirred it, then handed it back to Alma.

Because of Alma's age and possession of a large house, he had convinced young Alma and Ruth to move in with him. It had worked out well for all of them. Now Alma and Ruth had a son of their own. They had named him Helaman.

Alma sipped the sweetened chocolate, relaxing and enjoying his son's quiet companionship. Getting all the work done for Mosiah to ensure the smooth transition from kingship to a system of judges had taken much energy. He felt he had earned a rest.

They sat without talking. Alma felt very old, no longer able to do all the things he once did. He smiled to himself. If he tried to walk to Gideon or Melek now, they would probably have to pick him up on a blanket. He looked at his son. The younger Alma, his hair graying at the temples, was leaning forward, peering over the top of his cup at the floor.

"Father, I have spent much time in the past few years analyzing my life. I think some lessons can be learned from my rebellion. May I tell you some things about myself?"

His son's breaking of the silence startled Alma. He took a sip of the chocolate before answering. He leaned forward in his chair. "Speak up, son."

"Now that I have a son of my own, Father, I have attempted to analyze what happened in my youth—why I rebelled."

Alma looked at his son intently, his eyes sunken and almost hidden beneath his beetling gray eyebrows and bony cheeks.

The younger Alma spoke quietly. "As a child I watched as you helped people. You led people, not by your eloquence, but by your sincere conviction. I watched and listened and was deeply impressed. I learned before my teens that sermons did not come from mental discipline and wide reading alone—however essential these may be—but from life.

"I knew you loved me and wanted me to be part of your life. But your life was wrapped up totally in the church, and rather than be happy about that, I tried desperately to escape. I had strong feelings about freedom. I didn't want to be restricted. I didn't want to be fenced in like one of the goats I tended each day. I didn't want to be inhibited. I wanted to make my own rules. As the High Priest's son, I was constantly being watched, and I didn't like being watched."

Alma glanced at his son's face, seeing the look of wonder as young Alma apparently thought of his stormy past. As he started speaking again, Alma listened intently, knowing the depth of his son's feelings.

"Always gnawing at my mind was the faint suggestion that someday I would be called as High Priest. I tried to stifle such thoughts. No matter how good my home background was—no matter how insistent the call of God to my young heart—I determined to silence that inner voice and discover life for myself."

Alma remembered his own feelings of rebellion before the time of Abinadi.

The younger Alma continued. "To make sure I wouldn't be called to the priesthood, I went into warrior training. I'm not sure I really wanted to be a warrior or whether I just didn't want to be a priest. All this time, however, I had a suspicion the thing I was fighting was what I really wanted. I was all mixed up but unwilling to admit it—to myself or anyone else."

Alma was intent upon every word.

"I am so thankful to be where I am, and to know how narrow was my escape."

"Did the angel's appearance make it easier for you to be converted?"

"Perhaps. Conversion might have been easier for me because of the very awfulness of my sins. I knew exactly where I stood with God. I knew the depth of my sins. I knew my need for God. I was lost to the Church. Oh, I went to your sermons, and sometimes eavesdropped as you counseled other troubled people, but when I tried to tackle my own weaknesses, I seemed helpless . . . " He paused as he seemed to struggle for words. " . . . and I wouldn't come to you for advice."

"My son," Alma quietly prodded, "you were going to tell me why you rebelled in the first place."

The younger Alma sipped on his chocolate. At last he looked up.

"I think I felt religion was a weakness. So I rebelled. I took up with every symbol of rebellion. I became so weary of boredom and defeat that I even tried to run away from conscience. But thank God He would not let me kill my conscience. Even though I tried, He never let me go completely."

"You still felt doubt even while you were rebelling?"

"Oh, yes. God didn't leave me alone, though I wanted to be left alone. I thought often of your sermons and your counsel to me. While I walked between cities, I attempted stubbornly to put out of my mind the things I heard you say, but it was no use. God was always right there, and I was very uncomfortable. I didn't want Him to be that close. I felt as if the war between the Nephites and Lamanites was going on inside me."

Alma smiled understandingly. "What did you do?"

"With such inner turmoil, I came back to Zarahemla to hear you speak. You didn't even know I was here. I stood in back of the temple plaza and listened. There you stood—my ideal of a man.

"Even though you were speaking to the congregation, every word cut through me like a knife. I finally could take it no more and I walked away from the meeting to move restlessly through the streets. I shall never forget those moments."

Alma waited patiently as his son went back through painful memories. He reached over and put his hand on the younger Alma's arm.

"In that still summer evening, looking up past the trees into God's own sky, I actually shook my fist at the heavens and cried aloud, 'God, leave me alone.' "

Alma stiffened, jarred by his son's words.

The younger Alma continued. "I was shocked by my own defiant words. But I couldn't call them back. I felt cold inside. God's spirit had actually left me."

"Then what happened?" Alma asked. "Even though God had seemingly left my life, I was still not alone. I had my conscience. I struggled. I felt a deep sense of guilt which would not go away, no matter what I did. My conscience haunted me night and day, persisting in making me miserable. Fighting against the church and you seemed the only ways I could fight back against the feelings of my conscience."

"Did that help?"

The younger Alma smiled. "No, my conscience refused to be still. Like a small pebble in a sandal, it just irritated and cut."

Alma smiled as he asked, "And you didn't realize that at the time the only way to rid yourself of the irritating pebble was to take off the old shoe of rebellion?"

Nodding, his son continued, "I suppose it is human nature to fight against those things which we know to be right. We dislike admitting we might be wrong, or that we are doing wrong things. We operate behind a mask, trying to cover up, to camouflage. All the time I searched for peace of mind. I just searched in the wrong places." After a moment he added, "And with the wrong people.

"I opted for freedom, but what I found was slavery. I tried to remove the fences and the rules, but I found myself trapped behind fences of my own making."

"So rebellion led to sin?" Alma asked gently.

"I'm not sure. I think sin is just an attitude of rebellion," his son answered. "Sin caused a separation between me and you, and between me and God. It was a separation which had to be healed." He smiled. "God just chose a dramatic way to do it."

Alma felt weary, but he could not let such a golden moment pass by. He leaned forward intently. "Could you have done it without the angel?"

"I don't honestly know," the younger Alma replied. "Heaven only knows I had tried many times before. I didn't know how to break the power of wrongdoing. Each time I really tried to change, I failed. This led to discouragement and a drift further away from the truth."

Alma pursued his previous question. "I am still anxious to know that if you hadn't been visited by the angel, if you would have changed."

The younger Alma paused, apparently seeking a response. "Yes, the seeds of repentance were within me and were starting to grow. I was feeling pangs of guilt over what I was doing.

"I honestly believe that even without the angel I was ready for the fire of repentance to burn away my sins. It was only a matter of time."

Alma breathed a sigh of relief. "I am glad."

He took another sip of chocolate, then added, "Many people are in similar attitudes of rebellion as you had been. I don't think God will send angels to each of them. It has to be their decision to bring their own lives around and return to God's way so he can forgive them."

"That is true, but it is still difficult for me to realize I can be totally forgiven."

"May I remind you God forgave David, even though he had sinned greatly."

"But father, you don't realize what a sinner I was. I know God forgave David, but I feel I was much worse than David. What if my debt was just too big to forgive?"

Gently, Alma said, "Isaiah said, 'Though your sins be as scarlet, they shall be as white as snow; though they be red like crimson, they shall be as wool.' "

Breathing a sigh, the younger Alma said. "That helps, even though the hurt of what I have done remains with me."

Alma nodded. "You must first forgive yourself. It is basic to forgiving others."

"Father, you have taught the necessity of forgiving others, but even after forgiveness, won't they still feel some hurt?"

"Let me give an example. Suppose someone starts a false rumor about you, and it damages your reputation. Then the person realizes what he has done, that he has hurt you, and asks your forgiveness. You forgive him. Does that mean the hurt is gone, the damage undone? Does that stop the rumor from traveling on, continuing to do damage to your good name?"

Alma answered his own question. "No, it just means you love him enough to forgive him and bear the hurt yourself."

Nodding to himself, the younger Alma and sipped on his chocolate. "Father, I know you are tired, but thank you for helping me. I feel great relief. I can now advise my own sons and the people of the Church."

* * *

Mosiah's proclamation caused a stir throughout the land of Zarahemla. Earlier, he had asked the people whom they wanted to be their king, and now he published his long proclamation. Runners carried it to all parts of the kingdom where it was read and debated. Priests read it in the churches. Scribes read it to beggars in the streets. By Mosiah's signature, it was the law of the land. Upon his death, there would be no more kings in the promised land.

Chapter 17

An End and a Beginning

Throwing off his bedcovers, Alma swung his legs off the pallet. He grunted and strained, but try as he might, he couldn't raise himself to his feet.

"Almahah!" he shouted weakly.

"What is it, grandfather?" The quiet voice came from a dark-haired young man of sixteen who stood in the doorway munching on a wedge of bread.

"Get me out of this bed," blustered the white-haired old man. "It is the sabbath and I desire to go to church."

"But grandfather," started the youth.

"Don't 'but grandfather' me," declared the old high priest. "I am going to church. Help me to my feet."

Obediently, the boy stuck the bread in his mouth, and with both hands helped the old man to stand. Alma smiled. He was proud of all his grandsons, but Almahah was one of his favorites. In his mind he quickly reviewed his family.

Zoram and his two sons, Lehi and Aha, were serving as officers in the Nephite army. Ma'Loni was married and had two daughters of her own. Netta had two sons, Almahah and Abimolach, and two daughters, Lanetta and Shalu. Alma was convinced the girls were the prettiest in all of Zarahemla. Leesa, who lived with her husband, Abelon, in Melek, had no sons, but her three daughters, Kenra, Leesha, and Tonya, must be the prettiest girls in Melek. And now, very exciting to him, Alma and Ruth had a son. Helaman was still a tiny baby, but oh, what a beautiful baby. Ah, he thought, my life has been so full and now is so rewarding.

Alma leaned heavily on Almahah. What a strong grandson he was.

"Where do you think you are going?" scolded Netta when she saw her father. "You should be in bed."

"I have been in bed," he replied. "Now I am going to church."

Netta started to protest. The senior Alma smiled. "I am not planning to preach a sermon. I just want to see my friends and attend church one last time."

172

Alma was relieved when he saw that his daughter was not going to argue. He added quickly, "Almahah is strong. He can help me."

* * *

Excitement rippled through the congregation as the stooped Alma was helped to the bottom of the steps before the temple.

Alma listened intently as his son, Alma, the high priest, spoke of the father who demonstrated courage to "stand up for what he thought was right." He spoke of the man who "single-handedly thwarted the purposes of wicked king Noah." The high priest spoke of Alma's leadership in bringing the people from the Land of Nephi, then from the Waters of Mormon, and finally from the land of Helam to Zarahemla. Alma was almost embarrassed as his son heaped praises on him, comparing him to "Moses, who led the children of Israel from Egypt to the Promised Land."

After the service Alma stayed to visit old friends. A young mother brought her baby to him. "Please, would you just touch my baby?" Alma took the baby in his arms, chucked it lovingly under the chin, handed it back to the glowing mother. As he left, he leaned heavily on his grandson's arm, moving slowly and carefully down the steps.

At home once again, he listened as Abimolach and Almahah read and discussed King Benjamin's great sermon. Alma had read it hundreds of times, had used its concepts for sermons of his own, but as he heard the familiar words once again, tears filled his eyes.

That evening the family gathered to pay him respect. Zoram, Micael and their sons, Lehi and Aha, were there. Netta, who, since her husband's death, lived in Alma's house so she could take care of her aging father, was there with her four children. Leesa, Abelon and their three girls had come all the way from Melek to be part of the family gathering. Alma was there with Ruth and Helaman.

Alma looked around through eyes misted and shining. He dabbed at his eyes with wrinkled and bony hands. He held the baby, Helaman, on his lap, sensing rather than hearing the Lord's whisper: *This is he through whom the priesthood lineage will be carried.*

His children each visited with him, and, as he watched Zoram and his grandchildren, he thought back to the day they left the Waters of Mormon with Zoram carried on Helam's back.

Alma soon tired. He loved his children and grandchildren, but their constant noise and chasing did get on his nerves. He motioned for Zoram to take him inside. Netta fixed him a light supper. He pushed his food around the plate, finally forcing enough down to sustain himself. He relaxed in his chair, listening to the sounds of the children outside and the buzz of the adult voices.

What a lonely ten years it had been without Esther. How he missed her. He sighed. How fortunate he was to have his large family to watch over him in his old age.

He dreamily thought of family achievements. His son, Alma, was high priest, keeper of the records and chief scribe in the Church. Since Mosiah's proclamation to elect judges, the younger Alma had also been elected chief judge over all of the land. Alma smiled sleepily. He was glad to have his son carry the responsibilities.

He was equally proud of Zoram. His oldest son was captain over a Nephite army and Zoram's two sons, Lehi and Aha, were his chief lieutenants.

His girls were excellent wives and mothers. He could tell just by seeing their children. "Train them up in the way they will go . . . " He dozed as he tried to recall the verse from Solomon's writings.

He had not been idle during the past year. After he and Mosiah completed the translation of the Jaredite plates he worked with the king's scribes in disseminating copies to the people. He also helped Mosiah formulate his ideas on the system of judges and had read most of the scrolls of scriptures. He spent several days visiting with his old friend, Gideon, and just in the last week, at the invitation of his son, had spoken to a group of newly-ordained priests, challenging them to the work.

He sighed contentedly. I have lived a life of fulfillment, he thought. The Lord has truly been good to me. The scriptures are right: one cannot give without receiving an hundred-fold.

His head nodded as he fell asleep. Yet, it was as if he were not asleep. He seemed to be walking in a forest. He looked up at the trees. They were so different from the forests in the Land of Zarahemla or even in the Land of Nephi. The sky was purple-blue, with fleecy white clouds pirouetting across it. Trees, tall and magnificent, seemed to poke their heads right into the clouds.

His surroundings were unfamiliar, and yet he felt as if he had been here before. He walked through glens filled with flowers of every hue. Everything was so quiet and so peaceful. That was it! The peaceful feeling was similar to how he felt whenever the Lord spoke to him.

Ahead of him, forest opened into meadow. He stopped and gazed with rapture at the scene spread before him. The meadow was a sea of waving color. On the meadow's far side was a lake of the clearest blue imaginable—even bluer than the Waters of Mormon. Beyond the lake was a city, and what a city. Buildings stretched as far as he could see in every direction—buildings of pure white with roofs and steeples reaching to the cobalt sky above. It was a scene of grandeur.

His eye was attracted to movement in the field before him. The white of a woman's dress contrasted with myriad colors of flowers floating beneath her feet. Her dress swished as she walked quickly towards him. His eyes opened wide as he recognized that walk. He shook his head. Could it be? Esther? Forgetting his age he began to run. It was Esther! He ran faster through the meadow, his arms outstretched.

* * *

Esther stood in the air above the unconscious Alma, smiling with understanding. She said his name.

"Alma."

He stirred. She reached down and took his withered hand firmly in her two small ones.

"Alma."

She squeezed his hand in a way she had done hundreds of times.

His eyes slowly opened. He looked at her in wonderment and smiled, then reached for her. She beckoned, nodding her head. She let her eyes show how much she had missed him.

"Come, my love. The time has come for you to join me. You have done everything on earth which the Lord has desired of you. Come."

Alma stood, not feeling the years which usually slowed him so much. Esther led him forward, out of the room. He glanced back. An old man, head slumped back, sat in his favorite chair. Holding Esther's hand, Alma strode surely and quickly after her.

* * *

Netta came to visit with her father. She found him, drooped in his chair. She cried out. Alma and Zoram hurried in. There sat Alma, their father, a half-smile turning up his dry lips, sightless eyes open and staring.

Alma put his ear to his father's chest, then straightened up, a look of resignation on his face.

"He is gone," he said.

Leesa hurried in. When she saw her father's lifeless body, she dropped on her knees before him, grasping his cold hands in hers. She placed her cheek against his legs, rocking gently back and forth. When she looked up through her tears, it was with a soft smile.

She turned to Alma. "I feel mother's spirit here."

Alma nodded. "I, too." He paused, looking at the body of his father without really seeing it. Instead, he was seeing Alma, the high priest, teaching, baptizing, blessing people.

"He has finished his work," he said. "He has joined mother in the kingdom of his Father."

Epilogue

Mormon, a stack of gold plates before him, carefully inscribed his abridgment. So many times, he noted, fathers passed their faith and position on to children or a member of their family: Lehi to Nephi, Nephi to Jacob, Jacob to Enos, and so on. Now here was Alma passing the legacy of priesthood and responsibility to his son who was also named Alma. O, I only hope that my son, Moroni, will carry on my work, he thought.

He wrote, "And thus commenced the reign of the judges throughout all the land of Zarahemla, among all the people who were called the Nephites; and Alma was the first and chief judge.

"And now it came to pass that his father died, being eighty and two years old, having lived to fulfill the commandments of God.

"And it came to pass that Mosiah died also, in the thirty and third year of his reign, being sixty and three years old; making in the whole, five hundred and nine years from the time Lehi left Jerusalem. And thus ended the reign of the kings over the people of Nephi; and thus ended the days of Alma, who was the founder of their Church." Mormon put his stylus down. Looking at the sky, he remarked aloud, "Oh, that each of us had an angel to watch over us, as did Alma, the younger."

He shook his head in wonderment, and continued abridging and copying the plates which lay before him.